Advance Praise for *Longpath*

"This perceptive book is an antidote to nearsightedness. Ari Wallach won't just leave you planning months or years ahead—he challenges you to look generations ahead. Get ready to think and think again."

—Adam Grant, #1 *New York Times* bestselling author of
Think Again and host of the TED podcast *WorkLife*

"Reading this book is like joining hands across generations in order to find the hope, drive, and imagination necessary for us to build the world we wish to manifest. A world built on justice, spirit, and joy."

—Ai-jen Poo, president of the National Domestic
Workers Alliance and author of *The Age of Dignity*

"Ari Wallach has written an essential guide to the twenty-second century. You read that right. With the acumen of a futurist and the soul of a rabbi, Wallach shows us that the only effective antidote to the rampant now-ism of the present is to have an urgent conversation about reshaping the far future. *Longpath* will make every conversation you have more meaningful."

—Bruce Feiler, *New York Times* bestselling author of *Life Is in the Transitions*

"A brilliant futurist who sees with his whole heart, Wallach shows us how to co-create a future of dignity, justice, and love as daily practice. This book will ignite your agency and lift your gaze to the horizon of possibility. *Longpath* showed me how to feel future generations' joy—that joy is now my North Star. Wise, practical, powerful, this is an essential handbook for how to birth the world we dream."

—Valarie Kaur, bestselling author of *See No Stranger*
and founder of the Revolutionary Love Project

"People who face great oppression—as Ari's father did—are somehow best able to think beyond themselves, seeing ways forward just when every path seems blocked. Black people in America never had the luxury not to see ahead. We thank our ancestors at the same time we strive to become ancestors worth thanking. *Longpath* will help more people embrace this mindset and the behaviors that go with it. Changing our minds can transform our lives."

—Rashad Robinson, president of Color Of Change

"Like a prophet of old, Ari Wallach offers us an urgently needed message: While we can't thank those who came before us, our survival as a species relies on our paying their sacrifices forward. Wallach expertly combines evolutionary biology, psychology, and spiritual wisdom not just to remind us what we owe future generations, but to give us the tools we need to truly become better ancestors."

—David DeSteno, author of *How God Works*

"Ari Wallach will change the way you look at time. *Longpath* offers a thought-provoking perspective on how we carry our ancestral history and how we can shift our thinking from short-term reactions to long-term responses. What actions will we take if we view it from the perspective of our great-great-grandchildren?"
—Sharon Salzberg, author of *Lovingkindness*

"Ari Wallach's approach to being great ancestors is an antidote to the addled, unsustainable traps of short-term thinking. Philosophically deep and practical, timeless, and urgent, Wallach's message is one we need more than ever. Take it in; your descendants will be glad you did."
—Jamil Zaki, PhD, director of the Stanford Social Neuroscience Lab and author of *The War for Kindness*

"*Longpath* is a radical call to expand the window of our attention. In doing so, we shift our thinking and behavior, making us better, happier people."
—Amishi Jha, professor and author of *Peak Mind*

"By cultivating what Wallach designates the *Longpath* way of living, we have direction for how to get beyond short-term decision-making rooted in myopic opportunism. A poetic master of creative metaphor, Wallach invites us all to join in the *Longpath* journey, for species survival yes, but no less because this is a joyful and fulfilling way of living our lives together!"
—Daniel Liechty, author of *Facing Up to Mortality* and *Transference & Transcendence*

"I loved this book for its authenticity and audacity. *Longpath* not only helped me envision a brighter future but also to improve how I can be a more effective leader in the present. This is a playbook that anyone can leverage right now to achieve world-changing results. It's an impressive feat and makes *Longpath* a must read."
—Jonathan Greenblatt, CEO and national director of the Anti-Defamation League (ADL)

"Ari Wallach challenges practices that incentivize harming our future. Providing helpful tools and anecdotes, Wallach wisely guides readers into making personal and professional decisions with awareness of long-term impact—decisions that will enrich our being and one day make our far-off descendants proud."
—Ytasha L. Womack, author of *Afrofuturism*

"Like Viktor E. Frankl in *Man's Search for Meaning*, Ari Wallach gives us a road map to finding meaning and hope in this moment between what was and what will be with the deep insights and provocations one would expect from not just a futurist but a father who cares deeply about the world we will leave behind to our descendants."
—Alec Ross, *New York Times* bestselling author of *Industries of the Future* and *The Raging 2020s*

"Albert Einstein observed that we cannot solve our problems with the same thinking we used when we created them. Ari Wallach's *Longpath* provides a clear way to think differently so that we can better address the issues of our time."

—Jonathan Rose, author of *The Well-Tempered City*, cofounder of the Garrison Institute, and president of the Rose Companies

"What kind of world do we want our children and grandchildren to inherit? Ari Wallach refocuses us on this critical question, which our forebears once weighed more mightily than we do today. Becoming a great ancestor requires not only navigating ever-present crises but imagining the world as it could be through one's everyday philosophy and choices."

—Laurence C. Smith, author of *The World in 2050* and the John Atwater and Diana Nelson University Professor of Earth, Environmental, and Planetary Sciences at Brown University

"In a turbulent world, *Longpath* offers a moving, trenchant guide for anyone seeking to close the gap between the world as it is and the world as it should be."

—Hahrie Han, Stavros Niarchos Foundation Professor of Political Science, director of the SNF Agora Institute at Johns Hopkins University, and author of *Prisms of the People*

"Ari Wallach's *Longpath* is a timely reminder that even as acute challenges draw our attention, it is essential to take the long view if we are to achieve the shared vision of a just and sustainable world. At a time when resilience is an imperative, and not just a buzzword, *Longpath* provides a pathway to making it a reality."

—Aron Kramer, president and CEO at BSR

"In the context of a time that is hyperconnected yet fractured, filled with both transformational change and anxiety, Ari Wallach gives us a compelling road map forward, a manifesto for shifting our mindset from the short to the long term—bringing us from the past to the present to a better future we still have the chance to co-create, with even our smallest decisions and interactions."

—Asha Curran, CEO of GivingTuesday

"Brilliantly weaving together rationality and spirituality, *Longpath* offers a new lens through which we can all imagine and shape the future."

—Adam Bly, founder and CEO of System

"Ari Wallach has become our trusted guide to the future, and *Longpath* is our roadmap. *Longpath* is not a 'mindfulness time out,' but 'a frame of mind' for living. Wallach's storytelling gently and persistently moves us to realize that, like the butterfly whose flap of wings caused a storm miles away, our daily actions are building out the future for the generations to follow."

—Sudhir Venkatesh, William B. Ransford Professor of Sociology and African-American Studies at Columbia University

"What if we took the time to extend empathy and care to the generations that came before us? And how about generations that will come after us? In this heart-stretching, time-bending invitation, futurist Ari Wallach pushes us to widen our circle of concern by seeing ourselves as links on an intergenerational chain. Longpathism is a clarion call: it's on us to make sure the future of humankind is not characterized by the loneliness, alienation, and divisiveness we're living amidst today."

—Jenn Hoos Rothberg, executive director of the Einhorn Collaborative

"Sometimes all it takes to change your life is to see it from a different perspective. Ari Wallach's *Longpath* blows through conventional thinking and opens up a world where each and every one of us can carefully consider how the choices we make today can impact the future. If you are reconsidering your life choices, this book will illuminate the path forward."

—Kathryn Murdoch, cofounder and president of the Quadrivium Foundation

"When I hear the word 'futurist,' I expect jetpacks and meal-replacement pills. But Wallach isn't that kind of futurist. In this striking and insightful book, Wallach takes us back in time to see the *longer* picture. We emerge liberated from our small sense of time and endowed with the responsibility of being a future ancestor."

—Casper ter Kuile, author of *The Power of Ritual*

"A new framework for thinking about our decision-making patterns, with empathy at the center of all."

—Chade-Meng Tan, author of *Search Inside Yourself*

"Short-term thinking is enticing and may even feel good up front, but more often than not it ends up causing harm down the road. Wallach compellingly argues that our biggest challenges require playing the long game, and he shows us how to get started. We've got no time to waste."

—Brad Stulberg, author of *The Practice of Groundedness*

"*Longpath*—blending psychological, emotional, and even spiritual development—offers a crucial blueprint and inspirational call to action: to create the futures that we want for ourselves and our descendants."

—Hollie Russon Gilman, senior fellow at New America and affiliate fellow at Harvard's Ash Center for Democratic Governance and Innovation

"Written with brilliance, beauty, and no shortage of soul, *Longpath* is the most important and hopeful guide to the future we can start building today."

—David Sax, bestselling author of *The Revenge of Analog* and *The Future Is Analog*

This Book Belongs To:

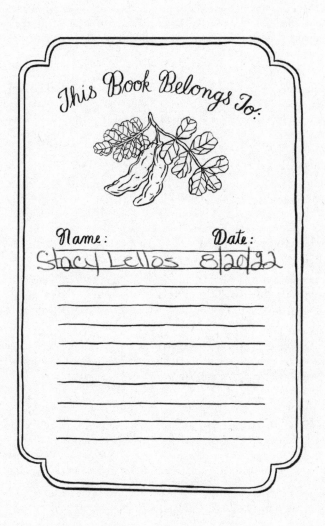

Name: Date:

Stacy Lellos   8/20/22

Longpath

Longpath

Becoming the
GREAT ANCESTORS
Our Future Needs

An Antidote for Short-Termism

Ari Wallach

HarperOne
An Imprint of HarperCollins*Publishers*

FIRST EDITION

Designed by Joy O'Meara @ Creative Joy Designs
Illustrations by Brooke Budner

Library of Congress Cataloging-in-Publication Data has been applied for.

ISBN 978-0-06-306873-5
ISBN 978-0-06-327588-1 (ANZ)

22 23 24 25 26   LSC   10 9 8 7 6 5 4 3 2 1

I strive to become a great ancestor to the multitudes
of generations to come, but above that,
I hope I have been a great father to my children—
Eliana, Ruby, and Gideon.

This book is dedicated to you and all
that you are and will become.

One day a man named Choni was walking along and saw a man planting a carob tree. Choni asked him, "How many years will it take until it will bear fruit?" He said to him, "Not for seventy years." Choni said to him, "Do you really believe you'll live another seventy years?"

The man answered, "I found this world provided with carob trees, and as my ancestors planted them for me, so I too plant them for my descendants."

—FROM THE TALMUD (TA'ANIT 23A)

Contents

Prologue   1

Chapter 1: Living
What Longpath Is and Why We Need It   5

Chapter 2: Changing
How What Worked Then Won't Work Now   37

Chapter 3: Practicing
Looking Backward, Inward, and Forward   59

Chapter 4: Creating
Futures and How We Make Them   97

Chapter 5: Flourishing
Working Together for a Better World   135

Epilogue   165
Longpath Megatrends   169
Journal Pages   171
Acknowledgments   179
Notes   183

Longpath

Prologue

At the heart of the city of Rome, Italy, stands the Colosseum. To this day, you can visit this iconic structure, marveling at the millions of cubic feet of travertine stone, stacked without mortar, that comprise its towering outer wall. You can stand where gladiators once stood and imagine the roar of more than fifty thousand cheering spectators. If you look up, you can see stalls that housed the members of the audience, completed in 80 AD. Most likely, the people filling those stalls shifted about in their seats, the hot sun beating down, snacking on chickpeas and drinking wine while waiting for the next spectacle. In the tunnels below, exotic animals paced and fighters—many slaves or criminals—awaited their fates. The smell of blood, sweat, and decay most likely permeated the bowels of the Colosseum, where the line between life and death neared its thinnest point.

We can go to this space and stand in the shadow of emperors and commoners, of women and men living very human lives. Fear and joy, hunger and satisfaction, stress and dreams all wove themselves into the lived experiences of these ancient Romans. Perhaps you can see some of yourself in them, or some of their legacies in you.

Now imagine the year 4020 AD. Hard to fathom, but it is the same distance *forward* in time that the gladiator age is *back* in time from my writing this in 2022. What will the inhabitants and visitors to Rome see then? What will they imagine about our lives today? Will they visit a soccer stadium and imagine the roar of fans? Will they pay an entry fee to view the remnants of a gas-powered Vespa scooter? Will they marvel at simulations of traffic dysfunctions that led an average motorist to lose 254 hours a year, trapped in a metal box with wheels? Will they recreate gelato recipes, using the "old ways"? Is pizza still a thing? What will they think about the problems we faced? Will they look at graphs showing extreme rises in temperatures or drought and resent us or be proud of us for the actions we took? Will they imagine the chaos of a global pandemic and feel confusion or empathy about our response? In a time that is sooner than we think, we will be their ancient past, their history. What will they write about us?

I love considering time in this way. While the Roman Colosseum is a big-picture example, you can create puzzles with time in ways that feel even closer to you. For those of you who are Gen X or older like me, imagine where you were in the year 1990—what did you think about? What did you wear? What music did you listen to? What were your most pressing problems? It doesn't seem that long ago, right? Now, if I do a little bit of math, I can tell you that today you are closer to the year 2050 than you are to 1990. In 2050, they will be listening to what you hear as "today's top hits" regularly on Spotify on a "golden oldies" channel. In case you didn't know already, the unimaginable future of yesterday is now here.

The book you're about to read will stretch time, your brain, and your heart so that you can become the great ancestors the future needs you to be. Together, we're going to explore how looking at time with a wider lens, coupled with our emotional and collaborative strengths, can make us great ancestors and help us in our own lives. We're going to look at 4020 A.D. and imagine the type of people that we want to be inhabiting the Earth, what they will care about, and how we can help them manifest their best lives by laying some foundations today. What's more, we're going to learn that this time—this very moment—is one of the best chances we have to make a huge impact on the lives of those to come. Let's get started.

CHAPTER 1 | LIVING

What Longpath Is
and Why We Need It

Look and listen for the welfare of the whole people
and have always in view not only the present but also
the coming generations, even those whose faces
are yet beneath the surface of the ground—
the unborn of the future Nation.

**—FROM *THE GREAT LAW OF THE HAUDENOSAUNEE*,
THE FOUNDING DOCUMENT OF THE IROQUOIS CONFEDERACY**

You might expect I'd start a book titled *Longpath* with a story about how every journey of a thousand miles starts with a first step. Or maybe you're expecting to read about the twenty-year journey to build the Transcontinental Railroad connecting the east and west coasts of America, or the two-hundred-year process of building the Great Wall of China, or maybe even something about "moonshots." Perhaps you expect a sermon on how we need to really, truly start acting on climate change, because there will soon be a billion climate refugees roaming the planet in search of shelter and water. I'll get to all of these in good time, but truth be told, the story of the future of human civilization often starts with something pretty innocuous. For instance, a buzz from a phone.

I was in the kitchen making my world-famous dragon eggs dinner (eggs scrambled with cut-up hot dogs and cheese) when I felt a vibration in my pocket. It was an app notification from our local school. My twelve-year-old daughter, Ruby, had missed turning in her Spanish assignment, which had been due exactly twelve seconds before. My instant reaction to that buzzing, though, was hundreds of thousands of years in the making. All sorts of chemicals and neurotransmitters started firing in my brain. Anger that she missed the assignment, sure, but beneath that was shame (*what kind of parent am I?*), fear (*if she keeps this up, she won't get into her choice of college*), and a deep-seated sense that by doing something wrong, I had upset members of the tribe and was going to find myself "pushed out" of the cave tonight, forced to fend for myself against large animals with very big teeth. With all this going through my mind and body, I had a choice to make: freak out, lose my shit, yell at Ruby, or pause . . . and follow the principles of Longpath.

Longpath—a simple but profound mindset that shifts thinking from the short term to the long term—allowed me to take that half-second pause and recognize the swirl of chemicals and hormones rapidly welling up inside me. And in that pause are the hundreds of thousands of years that came before that moment, the hundreds of thousands of years that would come after, and the awareness that I was just a link in a greater chain of being. I was, in my best impression of Carl Sagan, part of a pale blue dot in the ever-expanding universe of space and time. Half a second later, I realized that whether Ruby knew what *biblioteca* meant would not dictate her future or our collective humanity's future. What was most important was not getting worked up over the missed assignment—that would get resolved later after we had dinner and I could talk to her about it. What mattered was maintaining the balance of mental and emotional states of mind as we were about to sit down as a family—a ritual where how I connected with my loved ones would have a much greater ramification on Ruby's future than a single missed assignment. And then, even later, I'd do the most important thing: turn off those annoying phone notifications from her school.

We all have moments like these—probably more often than we realize. We live in a world of constant updates, notifications, and "breaking news," and these all conspire to spike our cortisol and adrenaline levels, elicit fight or flight responses from our central nervous systems, and—if poorly managed—send us spiraling down into a pile of smoldering emotional wreckage. This is the result of short-term, reactionary thinking, which, while valuable at times, can bubble over if it isn't kept in check. We lose sight of the larger whole—of what really matters to us in the big picture. The problem is that a short-term mindset (mindset being a set of beliefs that influences how you think, feel, and behave) gets triggered constantly, whether it's a distressing work email that intrudes late in the evening or the self-inflicted guilt that comes from a dad who feels he's not doing enough for his daughter in Spanish class.

These experiences are the new normal for so many of us, yet we face challenges that require us to go beyond this way of thinking and acting. There are moments when we need to think bigger than "right now" and think about a few hours from now, a few days from now, a few years from now, a few generations from now. The Longpath mindset works in part to help relieve our reactions to stressful moments by providing a way of seeing the world that cultivates future conscious thinking and behavior. Longpath helps us start thinking and feeling beyond our individual life spans and to the impact we will have on future generations. And yes, that previous generations have had on us.

But Longpath is more than a mantra, a handy "mindfulness time-out!" reminder, or a five-step prescription for a better tomorrow. It's a way to move about the world with the right frame of mind. It helps us prioritize the things that truly matter and recognize what doesn't. Longpath is a mindset, a way of being, and an approach to life and the universe that seeks out comity and union with all other living and nonliving things across time and space—taking a view from thirty thousand feet in the sky *and* thirty thousand years into the past and the future. Longpath reminds us that we are part of something bigger than ourselves, and that while our own time is finite, we need to become the great ancestors our descendants need us to be.

This risks sounding heavy and abstract, but Longpath can find expression in something as simple as a jogging track. My friend Michelle was part of a construction team building a new high school sports track and soccer stadium in her town. She felt a lot of pressure to finish the project on time and on budget. When a supplier came to her and explained that there was a new corn-based track surface material they could use, Michelle was about to reject it outright. It would last five times as long and had a lower carbon footprint in its manufacturing process, but it would cost much more and take a lot longer to lay down. She thought of the heat she might take if she agreed and of the installation deadlines and budgets her team had to hit to ensure their bonus.

Wait a second, she thought. What's the ultimate goal here? Make her bonus or build a stadium that would last, so that the next generations wouldn't have to start the work all over again? A delay and an earlier output of funds made much more sense than pushing something through so that she could be done with it and look good. She decided to at least try to make the better materials work.

When Michelle felt her initial impulse to reject the new material, and when I felt my initial impulse to hassle Ruby about her Spanish, we were doing what humans do: warding off a seemingly immediate threat, trying to fit in with the tribe, aiming to protect our short-term interests. But when we paused and considered the bigger—and yes, longer—picture, and our place within it, we were practicing Longpath. In time and with practice, that pause for Michelle, for me, ideally for all of us, gets shorter and shorter, until Longpath becomes the automatic way we think, react, and eventually shape the future.

A Rabbi Goes into West Point

My dad was born in Poland and orphaned after the Germans killed his parents during World War II. He became a forest-dwelling resistance fighter when he was just a teenager and often said in his heavily accented English: "If you forget the past, you don't have a future. What happens tomorrow started yesterday." I grew up grounded in this conception of time, and my kids know that they are alive today because of the decisions my dad made during World War II to resist and to fight. He said that to get revenge on Hitler, he didn't want to just kill Nazis— he wanted to have children and in turn grandchildren.

My dad's story looms large in my life, but it is only one piece of my heritage. My mother was an artist, an exceptional one, who studied under the futurist, systems thinker, and acclaimed design engineer Buckminster Fuller. A typical weekend day of my youth would see me at a San Francisco art museum with my mom, talking about the interplay of colors and texture and nuance while viewing a sculpture by Alexander Calder, and then we'd go home to my father's world, where we watched old World War II movies and were more likely to discuss the precepts of power from Sun Tzu's *The Art of War* than the shades of purple in a sunset. I lived in a home that existed in separate times—a dad who, while extremely social and intelligent, could never fully escape the trauma of the 1930s and '40s, living in the "what was," and a mom who was modern and lived in the "what could be." A typical dinner conversation would therefore usually span back and forth between the 1920s and the 2120s. And there I sat, in the in-between.

As a result of my yin and yang upbringing, my life was a

series of seeming contradictions. I went from wanting to attend the US Army's academy at West Point to studying Peace and Conflict Studies at UC Berkeley. One semester, I lived in Washington, D.C., and split my weekdays between working for the Clinton-Gore reelection campaign and the United States Institute of Peace, and then spent my nights and weekends absorbing the dialogues of the Indian philosopher Krishnamurti. After graduation, I spent workdays strategizing for dot-coms in the newly booming Silicon Valley and weekends learning and meditating at Green Gulch, a Zen center in Marin County.

A pattern emerged in these experiences: whether I was mediating disagreements as the head of conflict resolution for UC Berkeley's co-op housing system or trying to help a dot-com focused on women's leadership, it seemed the way we aimed to solve problems only touched the surface of what the problems really were. An argument about the co-op kitchen directors spending money on fancy shellfish, for instance, was less about dollars or a decision-making procedure than it was about the values and baggage everyone brought to the subject of wealth and privilege. A dot-com trying to support women in leadership was all about shiny "tool kits" and "HR tips," but the real problem—and thus, the real support needed—lay in a much more deeply entrenched patriarchal system that did not offer family leave, quality childcare options, or equal pay. In short, the problem-solving frames we'd become habituated to didn't account for the past, the future, or the myriad political, emotional, and psychological factors at play. It's not like I was the only one who'd noticed this, but we all—myself included—felt powerless when it came to the big stuff. We all wanted, or at least felt we needed, quick short-term solutions just so we could "move on." And so, we played checkers when we needed to be playing 3D chess.

I continued to see people playing the wrong game, so to speak, throughout my career. By 2015, I ran a business consultancy (but in true yin-yang fashion, only after seriously considering rabbinical school) helping leaders across the corporate, philanthropic, and governmental realms think and act strategically. More and more of my clients were only looking to create impact in the here and now, often unknowingly at the expense of future generations. This came to a head when I was in Geneva speaking with some of the top thinkers and doers in the global refugee response sector. When I pressed them about what we should be doing about the coming waves of climate refugees, they responded they couldn't think about that because the house was on fire *now*. They were also beholden to their bosses, they explained, who didn't prioritize the (non-voting and non-donating!) future, and a twenty-four-hour news cycle that was on their backs about what they were doing this very instant. They only had so many years left in the job and on this earth, and they could only do what they could do.

I kept pushing that while we couldn't sacrifice the needs of the present, we had to find a way to look at the present and the future as one whole continuum, otherwise we were doomed to be Sisyphus, pushing a boulder interminably uphill just to have it roll back down when we were almost at the top. They looked at me blankly. I knew then that the short-term thinking, and the separation of the business and moral worlds that this conversation made so clear, had to be addressed before we could make any positive, lasting change.

A variation of the conversation occurred soon after, when I was invited to speak at 10 Downing Street in London. I had ostensibly been brought in to talk to decision-makers about innovation and how governments might best meet their citizens' needs in the twenty-first century. Yet coming off these unsettling meetings in Geneva and others like it, I decided to tweak my remarks at the last minute and talk about "how to meet the needs of British citizens in the *twenty-second* century." I wasn't met with blank stares this time. The audience understood my message but argued they'd never get buy-in from their constituents. Voters wouldn't care about the far future, because they had been trained their whole lives to look for immediate results from their governments—a by-product of the election "business cycle" where you start running for your next election the day after you win your last one.

My critics in Britain weren't wrong. A new manual was needed, one that would offer instruction on *how* we all—not just leaders—could think about the world and our purpose in it differently and *why* it matters. So, on the success of a well-received TED talk, a very understanding wife, and some close friends who believed in me, I started Longpath Labs. Longpath Labs is an initiative focused on bringing the Longpath mindset and behaviors to people, organizations, and societies. I've brought Longpath to the leadership at places like PBS, Facebook, and Twitter, who have shown curiosity about what it might look like to increase empathy, and the overall health of their community's conversations, over time. Longpath Labs officially launched in 2016, when I started jotting down notes for the book you now hold in your hands.

This is the book I was born to write: It's the culmination of the seemingly disparate threads of my life that seem to have no business existing in the same human being. I am considered a futurist, but instead of talking about technology-driven predictions of tomorrow's world, I start by talking about the past. Most often, the very deep past. I bring together multiple disciplines because that's exactly the approach we need to tackle today's problems. I draw from the fields of neuroscience, evolutionary biology, art, social systems, history, religion, and psychology. Perhaps most significantly, I take an approach that brings *all* of our abilities and senses as humans to bear. We don't just need our brains and our brawn, we need a capacity for self-insight, trust, cooperation, and a mix of big-sky visioning with pint-sized actions. And let me grab my megaphone for this one: We absolutely cannot talk about the future without inviting emotion, intuition, and awe back into our lives and our decision-making. We have to be full-spectrum human beings who can go forward, backward, and inward. This is why at the center of the Longpath insignia is the motif of a dragonfly. Dragonflies don't have two eyes, but actually thousands of mini-eyes that can see equally well in all directions. Dragonfly vision is a core element of Longpath living.

Emotion: The Queen of 3D Chess

Let's go back for a moment to my friend Michelle. She was about to reject the better, hardy material for the sports stadium based purely on the numbers her analytical brain could run through. Her decision had emotional influences, though: What about the fact that she didn't want to feel she'd failed her team? Or the discomfort in the pit of her stomach that she was putting immediate payoff for a few before longer-term payoff for the many? It may be that, after inviting her emotional side to the discussion, she'd give the analytics more weight. We live in a world where tradeoffs are sometimes necessary, after all. But it wasn't her impulse to even *consult* her feelings or motivations on the subject. When it comes to so many of our decisions, feelings are deemed irrelevant at best, counterproductive at worst. And so, we have long pushed them away.

The sidelining of feelings is nothing new in Western culture.

In ancient Greece, the Stoics made suppressing emotion an art form. Aristotle, the grandfather of the scientific method, once described the passions as capricious, dangerous roadblocks on the path to becoming fully human. But I think it's fair to say that "feeling" really fell out of favor during the Enlightenment, or the Age of Reason, when philosopher René Descartes decided to rip the mind and body in two, and "rationality above all" became solidified in the Western consciousness. Remember, Descartes wrote *I think, therefore I am,* not *I feel, therefore I am!* You also had big-time philosophers like Immanuel Kant running around proclaiming that nothing was higher than reason and Thomas Paine dismissing debate outside the sphere of reason as the equivalent to giving medicine to the dead. Ouch. Rationality was the golden ticket. Francis Bacon, who played a pivotal role in advancing the scientific method, once wrote, "It is impossible to love and be wise." Even the *poets* were brought over to the rational side, for Pete's sake, as Alexander Pope eulogized:

Nature and nature's laws lay hid in night;
God said, "Let Newton be," and all was light.

To be fair, a lot of very good things came from the focus on scientific progress and a concentrated focus on the quantifiable, without which many of us would not be here. I personally probably wouldn't have lived past a burst appendix at age eighteen without medical advancements that can be traced to the Enlightenment. But somehow, we threw out the baby with the bathwater; we tossed out any respect for our emotional lives. Emotions and "being emotional" became viewed, like our appendix, as nonessential organs. Western cultures adopted beliefs that led us to stifle the attributes within us that are socially ascribed to the feminine—things that we've been conditioned to see as lesser—like our empathy, our compassion, and our intuition. Our heroes, real or imagined, were characters like Sherlock Holmes, Charles Lindbergh, and Napoléon Bonaparte—men, usually, who were analytical, stoic, and seemingly void of emotion. What's more, anyone displaying high emotions (usually women) was clinically diagnosed as "hysterical." (*Hysteria,* in fact, originates from the Greek word for "uterus.") We got to the point where we had to dub an entire group of people—born during the Great Depression and World War II—the "Silent Generation" because their collective emotional trauma had no avenue to air itself out. More recently, we've seen an American marketing company creating a "snowflake test" to weed out overly sensitive job candidates and bumper stickers touting, "Nobody cares. Work harder."

That just won't do for the times we face, which will require us to draw on all our faculties. If we discount emotion, we're like Batman going into a firefight with just his batarang. Everyone knows that when combined with Wonder Woman and her lasso of truth, this dynamic duo is unstoppable, much greater than just the sum of their parts.

That's why Longpath brings emotions back to the fore. Because while sci-fi future-thinking is cool, what will really drive action toward creating the world we want into reality is how that vision lets you feel. Emotions are shortcuts that can be harnessed to guide us toward rational choices and coopera-tive action. They can be geared toward long-term thinking and behavior, and they are essential if we're to imagine a possible future. Empathy—our connection to other people's thoughts, emotions, and well-being—motivates us to act positively on behalf of others. So—and I'll get into this more in coming chapters—while thinking about saving for retirement is help-ful, truly feeling and sensing the contented emotions of living that retired life is what will help you actually put money away. Cold rationality may help you win a fight with your spouse, but leaning into the feelz you want to have with your partner over the next few decades helps you rethink what "winning" the ar-gument really means. Emotions are integral to Longpath, and you'll notice I return to them again and again throughout the book. Note that emotions aren't good or bad: The point is to use them productively and wisely.

I also want to pause here for a moment to acknowledge that it takes an enormous amount of privilege to be able to think this way. Those who live on the margins, who are one illness or missed paycheck away from losing access to basic safety and security or who are living in oppressed conditions are often too busy surviving to think beyond their next meal or how to avoid impending abuse. The right decision is usually the one that gets them to the next day. But even those who have been historically excluded from influencing the future can learn to Longpath. You don't have to be a 3D chess master to learn the basic moves. In fact, I'm sure you can think of countless stories of actions that someone living on the edge has made for the love of their family or their community. They tap into their emotions, dig deep, and take action toward a better future for themselves and those to come. It's Longpath 101—an attuned resourcefulness and emotional resilience, big or small, that can be of benefit to not just one person or generation, but to the future at large. What's more, this type of altruism and emotional connection has the potential to make exponential, systemic impacts during historic periods of chaos and complexity—one of which we happen to be in right now.

Intertidals: Why We Need Longpath More Than Ever

In the late summer of 2020, five months into the coronavirus pandemic, my family decided at the last minute to run away for the week. My three kids' bickering had accelerated by the day, and we were all dealing with cabin fever. The kids needed an infusion of nature and an extrusion from walks around the block that had become so routine they had memorized the number of rocks and trees in neighbors' gardens—and, alarmingly, had started naming them. We found a last-minute deal on a week at a beach house and went for it.

On our first evening, the five of us stood together at the ocean's edge. As the waves came in, the water brushed our ankles. As the waves went out, the sand shifted beneath our feet. As anyone who has ever stood on a shoreline knows, it's a strange feeling. You're still standing, but there's an unsteadiness. The sand beneath you is giving way and yet you do not appear to be moving. Your macule, a tiny bundle of hair wrapped in calcium crystals located in your inner ear and responsible for your sense of balance, is telling you that something's happening, something's moving. But when you look down at your feet you don't necessarily see it.

The sand washing away was a moment of punctuated equilibrium—a rapid change after a long period of stability—and a perfect stand-in for how we were all feeling that summer. In reality, it's how we'd all been feeling the past few years. Even my eight-year-old, Gideon, was keenly aware that his old life of camps and school and playdates and extended family vacations was gone. It would be replaced by something else—maybe even something better—but what?

The human experience is like this—it changes and fluxes

all the time, but sometimes there seems to be a burst of radical transformation that happens all at once and on many different fronts. On a grand, historic scale, there have been a handful of periods of dramatic transition that not only mark changes in our behaviors and environments, but that also reset the defaults of how we think and operate as human beings—windows like the Agricultural Revolution, the Middle Ages, the Scientific Revolution, the Enlightenment, the Industrial Age. Oh, and *now*.

I call these periods of flux *Intertidals*. An intertidal zone, when talking about the ocean, is the in-between place where the ocean meets the land that is sometimes under water and sometimes exposed to air between low and high tides. It's a place of both crazy creativity and crazy danger. Barnacles survive by anchoring themselves to rocks for stability, mussels by holding seawater in their shells to keep from drying out during low tides. Not every organism can adapt or keep up with these constant changes, and so an intertidal is considered an extreme ecosystem.

This is why Longpath is so important right now: We are in the midst of an Intertidal period of rapid change. All around us we see that old ways of being and doing no longer work. Worldwide, across the institutions of media, religion, government, business, and NGOs, complex interactions have increased, but trust has fallen to historic lows.[1] Global challenges like climate change, pandemic disease, financial crisis, and tech disruptions are exploding and are on a collision course with fragmented geopolitical structures and citizens.[2] Around 150 million people fell out of the global middle class in 2021, the first time that demographic has shrunk since the 1990s.[3] Whereas once we took for granted that the next generation would be better off than we are, people increasingly feel that they and their families will be worse off in five years.[4] The *way* we work has changed, with one-third of the American workforce now participating in the gig economy and automation infiltrating almost every sector.[5] We even have the capacity to edit our genetic code now in a way that gets passed down to our kids and their kids and so on—but we're not having conversations about that outside of the pages of *The Atlantic* or high-mountain retreats of thought leaders.

Meanwhile, we also see new, positive ways of thinking, doing, behaving, and organizing popping up. We have sites like Buy Nothing that endorse a different, circular kind of nonconsumptive economy, and mass social movements challenging the active and residual legacies of white supremacy, colonialism, and patriarchy in society. We see previously unconnected strangers pitching in to fund microloans, creative projects, or a family's medical expenses. But these emerging dynamics are still nascent, often scattered, and seem to be susceptible to collapse in rapidly evolving times. In other words, the old ways are dying hard deaths, but the new ways are still in the process of being born, and being in the in-between can sort of suck. But the in-between is also where all the creative juice is—and for those of us who want to push the envelope of who we are as human beings, it's our time to shine.

Many people ask me what makes an Intertidal special and why they should care. We experience small paradigm shifts all the time within a given industry or culture (the printing press, the Model T, the rise of civil rights, the tearing down of Cold War walls, the Internet), but life seems to carry on with some degree of normality. An Intertidal occurs when those paradigm shifts are heightened and intertwined, when the degree of complexity and confusion in our lives is turned up to eleven, and, most important, the underlying ideas, narratives, and rules of what it means to be a human being are called into question.[6]

Intertidals are not always brought on by a collapse. They are big shifts that can be brought on by things like mass population growth (because we're all living longer), mass migration, mass urbanization, mass climate change, and mass die-offs. When we look at our present moment, we can check off all of those boxes on the Intertidal checklist. Technology usually doesn't go on this list because it typically isn't a *cause* of a transformation; it merely adapts to and accelerates transformation. I would say the exception, though, is now. Technologies like CRISPR, AI-enhanced brain implants, or artificial uteri have the potential to fundamentally change what we mean when we say *Homo sapiens*. We're not experiencing an Intertidal tremor, in other words—what we have here is an earthquake. And this might be the Big One. What happens next will decide the fate of the entire species.

Moments of disorder like these offer a distinct opportunity for transformation *if*, like the barnacles and mussels that thrive in an oceanic intertidal, we know how to use all of our faculties. Nobel Prize–winning complexity theorist Ilya Prigogine found that when systems are at their most chaotic, they have the capacity to suddenly shift into an inordinately high degree of order and equilibrium.[7] Small changes can have big effects. Think of this like a murmuration, when birds that are scattered every which way suddenly come together in an organized formation with grace and purpose. This Intertidal moment, in which our long-held norms and narratives are coming into question, can be the breeding ground for exponentially evolved human thinking and behavior. We can navigate this moment of chaos and build societies that relish human and ecological flourishing. But it's not a foregone conclusion that we will.

Around twelve thousand years ago, there was a significant Intertidal: the first Agricultural Revolution. The climate stabilized and humans began working with the land surrounding them, which meant they stuck around in one place, and, in time, the first "real" civilizations came about. Humans adapted and created more developed, complex ways of being and perceiving—they gave our species an operating system upgrade. Our Agricultural Age ancestors went from worldviews that were built upon the experiences of small, tight bands of hunters and foragers ("keep moving, eating, and do your best to stay alive!") to new realities informed by life within larger and larger social groups, including the need for rules, systems, and guiding narratives (Hi, God!) to manage this growth. *That* Intertidal period led to an evolved way of life. (Though one could argue that cubicles might not be so evolved, I'll go with the invention of penicillin and my daughters' right to vote any day.)

But change for the better isn't the guaranteed outcome for Intertidals. When the mighty Roman Empire collapsed, for instance, Western civilization fell into chaos. If we look closely, we can see that it had been building for a while. A climate optimum ended, ecological pressures forced foreign groups like the Goths and Huns to invade, plagues and infectious diseases killed people off at astonishing rates, infertility became a huge barrier to recuperating population numbers, soil was depleted, and the economic spoils and plunder of foreign lands dried up as military expansions slowed.[8] And, as is the case in such periods of disorder, many people looked toward a strong voice—with a good, all-encompassing story—to fill the void of uncertainty. In this case, the Roman Church stepped in. From a civilizational perspective, the Church's rule (I'm talking power and politics here; not theology) marked a huge contraction—the onset of the Middle Ages. This is what happens when Intertidals go bad, when people don't or aren't able to claim their full power as co-creators in what comes next.

So which way are we going to go now? Are we going to come apart, like after the fall of Rome, or help each other, like during the Agricultural Revolution? Since the end of the Middle Ages, our underlying story has been that humans can know, navigate, predict, control, and colonize the world and the future if they leverage the right knowledge for what is deemed as "progress" by the people of that era. What will our new story be? Can we build a story of progress that embraces an inclusive, psychologically evolved, and ecological objective, which by its very nature hooks future generations up with what they'll need to flourish? Put simply, can we make a better *us*? Can we be the great ancestors that future generations need us to be?

YOU HAVE PROBABLY NOTICED there is a book plate on the inside cover of this book. My hope is that this book can serve much like family bibles have for centuries. While bibles tend to record days of birth, marriage, and death, my hope is that you might use this book to record your values, regrets, and aspirations for your descendants. You can answer the questions I ask throughout this book in the journal pages, starting on page 173. You can make it a generational playbook for your family, or, if you're reading this from your office desk, why not sign your name and give it to the next person who takes your position in the future?

To begin, note that the scope and scale of the Intertidal can be hard to wrap your head around, let alone your feelings. Let's try to bring things down to size a bit. Think about a major change in your life that had a Before, an After, and an undefined Space-Between. Maybe it was the birth of a child, a move to a new city, an accident, a significant illness, or the death of a person who was important to you. How did it feel to have your world turned upside down? How long did you spend in denial or avoidance? Did you find it easy or hard to adapt to your new understanding of the world and your place in it? What did you have to let go of? What did you discover? Did you ever feel resistant? Did you feel scared or excited? Was it painful or joyful or numbing? Did you experience any conflicting feelings or ideas that felt equally true at the same time? What helped you cope? Did people try to give you "expert advice" even though they had no way of knowing what you were going through? Did all the upheaval eventually settle down into new patterns and habits? Did you have a hand in determining what your new norms would be? Was this "new normal" healthy or unhealthy for you? What about for those around you? Was there something you could have done better if you had to do it all over again?

Now imagine that everyone you know (and don't know) is having many major life events all at the same time (even if they don't want to admit it) and that how well they navigate this change will ripple out and set the stage for generations to come. Whoa, right? Welcome to the Intertidal.

The Choice We Face Now

Here we each stand—barefoot and vulnerable—in the Intertidal zone. There are two paths to take: one that appeases our short-term, reactionary self (*this is uncomfortable, get me out of here!*) and one that appeases our long-term, empathetic thinking (*this is uncomfortable, let's figure out how to avoid this suffering now and in the future*). The first is characterized by our brain's limbic system, which controls the amygdala, the seat of our fear response, and neurotransmitters like dopamine, part of the reward system of the brain. It is because of the limbic system that we get a rush of adrenaline if someone threatens us, that we jump at every notification from our smartphone like Pavlov's dogs, and that we struggle to connect big ideas like climate change to our little, everyday decisions that are contributing to it. Short-term thinking is necessary, but not all the time. The key is knowing when to put short-term thinking in time-out.

The second path forward is a recognition that while our brains are wired for fight or flight, they are also wired for cooperation and prospection (aka thinking ahead). Humans tend to thrive in social, collaborative settings, and we are able to conceive and prepare for future scenarios. Cooperation and prospection are our superpowers. Behind them is a different pattern of comprehension: empathy and long-termism. We are capable of imagining and having conversations about what we want, where we are going, and how to get there.

To harness these superpowers, we need a new collective and democratic story, based on a foundation and vision of where—and who—we want to be. Our current cultural narrative prioritizes the immediate and the reactionary, which doesn't have a clear end goal. Yet in order to reimagine our roles within the larger whole—of other beings and fellow humans now, and of future generations—we must ask ourselves: Where are we going? I often answer this question by thinking about the symbolism of the Holy Land in the story of Exodus: When the Hebrews left Egypt and wandered through the desert, the vision of a land flowing with milk and honey, a Holy Land to come, kept them going. Where, or what, is our Holy Land? And is it just a *place*, or might it also be a way of being? We need to wrestle with these questions about the future we want—as opposed to the one that just washes over us—and we need to do it together.

We need to focus on a vision of the future that's very much about the humans we want to be—the prosocial, intergenerational way of being and feeling in the world that we spread through our everyday actions. It *is* possible to instill a sense of meaning and purpose in others and the world through our behavior and our decisions. I have three children—Ruby, Eliana, and Gideon—and, guesstimating the average number of children in each generation, I might have around eight thousand descendants two hundred years from now.[9] *Eight thousand* beings with a portion of me—and I mean that in a broad sense—within them will make their own contributions to this world. It's not that I think something I say or do at home on a Tuesday night will directly dictate the actions of my great-

great-grandchild on a Tuesday night in 2154. But it does play a significant role in terms of how we shape the near and even distant future. I am passing on important values, thought processes, stress level responses, communication skills, and problem-solving approaches that, put together, my kids will absorb and that will guide their own decisions and interactions with others. In short, when it comes to the big picture, how I show up for my kids matters.

Likewise, how we vote, where we spend our money, what decisions we make from the family room, to the boardroom, to the situation room, even to the bedroom, matter. How we all show up in our encounters with friends, coworkers, and even strangers matters. The way we say hello to others, how we react during an argument with our partner, and even how we listen to that voice in our head impacts not just the now, but people thousands of years from now. You've probably heard of chaos theory, which claims that small ripples—even a butterfly flapping its wings—can have large effects on weather patterns thousands of miles away. My argument is that the same is true on an individual level and across time. We can harness this belief that small actions have great effects; we can be intentional about it.

What it all boils down to is that we have some decisions to make. Do we want to stay with the short-term, amygdala-in-control thinking and acting that represents so much of our approach to life today? Live our lives and then who cares? There are some—many, actually—who will say yes to those questions. They don't care much about where this whole humanity road ends up, because their time will have passed. While I wish no ill will on those folks, this book is probably not for them. This book is also probably not for those who want to see us transition away from the human body with all of its foibles to something more "silicon," a version of humanity that is essentially uploaded and only exists on the cloud. In fact, it's the foibles, the emotions, the warts (literal and figurative) that make us who we are in all our imperfectness. If we were uploaded and perfect, what fun would that be?

Most of us, though, don't dismiss the importance of future generations. And most of us don't want to be silicon. Instead, most of us want to have a sense that we are part of something much bigger—and in fact, research shows that's what makes us more content in our lives. For example, in a study of 132 countries, those with the greatest sense of meaning also had the highest rates of religiosity.[10] But religion has fallen out of popularity. The percentage of those who have no religious affiliation—known as "Nones" for the way they mark surveys about their beliefs—is at the highest rate ever. Nearly half of young adults (aged eighteen to twenty-four) have no religious affiliation at all. Yet all of us, even the "unchurched," have questions about meaning and life's big questions. The problem is, when we don't have the shared frameworks or religious texts that we used to have, we struggle to comprehend and process big ideas like ethics and purpose. So where do we turn to understand our role in the bigger picture?

Longpath can be a common story for the religious and nonreligious alike. It can be a framework for a conscious social evolution, one that is about knowing ourselves *and* seeing ourselves within a much bigger narrative. And in the process, it can give us solace and a sense of psychological safety during unsettling times. Longpath offers a sense of purpose in that you're collectively imagining a new vision of the "land of milk and honey" that can nourish you today as well as future generations, and you can start your journey there this very second. And it gives you a sense of meaning in your own life, and in the way you touch others, because it emphasizes a crucial truth: How you care for this moment—right now—matters. It matters today, tomorrow, and yes, thousands of years from now.

To get started, we have to relearn some things. Because our old ways? As you'll see in the next chapter, they just won't work anymore.

How What Worked Then
Won't Work Now

The greatest revolution of our generation is
the discovery that human beings, by changing
the inner attitudes of their minds, can
change the outer aspects of their lives.

—WILLIAM JAMES

As a consultant to major institutions ranging from the United Nations to Facebook, I would sit down with people and say, "Let's talk about your future," and they'd respond, "Great, I'm willing to look far out—like, even eight months!" Lest you think those folks are outliers, dig deeper and you'll see their response is pretty normal.[1] These are not bad people, or unintelligent people. They're just human beings living in a system that rewards short-termism: an impulse to seek rapid solutions and rewards.

We are all guilty of short-termism. For instance, let's say you're looking to buy a house. Your realtor shows you a new development where the construction is solid and the neighborhood schools are stellar. You're won over by the large yard and stately front porch, and you are elated that you can actually afford it. Your offer is accepted, and you move in. A few years later, a big storm hits and your house is in danger of flooding. You throw as many sandbags as possible in the way of the rising water. But that doesn't get at the deeper problem, which is that your home is built on a floodplain (why was the development allowed to be built there in the first place?), or that global warming is putting your home at risk not just today but for the next series—no, *decades*—of storms. Still, the sandbags work, your home is saved, and you forget about the problem until the next storm. I call this a sandbag strategy, and folks—including me—use it everywhere. ("Gideon, finish your broccoli if you want dessert!" "Hey Ms. CEO, buy back those stocks to increase the share price. Your bonus will rise, never mind what it means for long-term investment in your workers!")

This scenario highlights the many layers of short-termism working against us. The blocks we face as humans happen at the neurological level ("I'll be happy if I live in this shiny, beautiful house!"), at the societal level ("As a grownup, I should really own a home."), and at the level of the systems we've created all around us ("The schools in this neighborhood are great, so if I buy here, my kid will get higher test scores."). But throughout this home-purchasing and home-saving process, you didn't realize all that was going on below the surface. In fact, somewhere between 80 to 95 percent of our decision-making happens this way, and we have to own that truth before we can do anything else.[2] Yet, short-termism isn't exactly a sexy issue to bring attention to. There aren't marches for ending short-termism, or wristbands showing your solidarity with Longpath. No celebrity is going to take it up as their cause, because we all are guilty of it in one form or another, and no one wants to be called a hypocrite. But as this chapter and the subsequent ones show, we don't need to be perfect to take on short-termism or to start building better futures. Flawed as we are, we can still fight to become better humans, and to craft a better humanity.

Our Short-Term Minds

There is a reason we often think short-term: Even though we live in a time with a "humans shall inherit the earth and have dominion over nature" narrative, we are all—every last one of us—basically very evolved apes. This means that there are biological hurdles in front of us as we pursue a shift from short-term to long-term thinking and acting. Understanding this will help us recognize some of our instincts, but also what we're capable of when we outgrow those ancient habits and start cultivating new thought processes.

At some level, short-termism is a good thing, a response our hunter-gatherer ancestors needed to survive. If you were walking along thirty thousand years ago and saw a bunch of berries, you didn't just eat a couple and presume more would come eventually. You ate everything you could possibly fit into your stomach, because at an instinctual level you understood you needed to take immediate advantage of what was in front of you.

So it's not that short-termism is completely villainous. The problems arise when we start building in incentive structures so that we carry short-termism on in our daily life at the expense of our future self, and—perhaps most important—the expense of future generations. The problems expand because Intertidals heighten our short-term impulses. Remember that a hallmark of these chaotic periods is systems breaking down—and when we truly feel out of control, we seek immediate safety. We want to feel stable. So we seek whatever ultra-short-term fixes will provide that. We run from the tiger instead of stopping to read the book *What to Do When Chased by a Tiger*. We let the wiring that compelled us to grab the berries in the Serengeti drive our every decision.

Our short-term tendencies are getting worse, and not just because we're in an Intertidal—we're also stuck in a hamster wheel of presentism. I happen to be friends and neighbors with Douglas Rushkoff, who writes about this phenomenon—among other topics—for a living. While most neighbors sit around comparing lawns, Douglas and I sit and fret about whether the plastic-sided pool we erected for our kids to share during the pandemic summer will outlast civilization, and whether buying the pool in the first place hastens that end. Presentism, Douglas often says, is what comes after futurism. "Where we spent a century or more leaning forward toward the future," he wrote, "addicted to growth, and speculating on whatever might be next, we are now in an era that empha-sizes the present. The here and now."[3] He's not referring to the Buddhist understanding of the here and now, but rather a Hall of Mirrors version of it, where everything happens at once, and *now,* and where there is no history or future. And even more insidious is how presentism robs us of our ability to truly imagine a different world, a different tomorrow. When there is no past or future and just The Now, we become complacent and accepting of *what is* and lose our ability to even ask "How might we?"

A great way to visualize this, courtesy of Douglas, is an analog clock versus a digital clock. If you even have access to an analog clock, look at it. You see the whole day laid out before you. You see the relationship of six to nine. You see the seconds ticking away, moving you forward in time millimeter by millimeter. But with a digital clock, you only see the exact time that it is, right now. It's not part of something bigger, it just *is.* The problem with this, of course, is, well, what a bummer. Imagine all that we don't see when all we can see is right in front of us. When we can't actually see that we're just specks in the grand scheme of time.

The rapid pace of technological development, particularly when untethered to ethics, exacerbates presentism, heightening our short-term tendencies. Take schools and grading, for instance. When I was a kid, my report card came in the mail twice a year, leading to a conversation with my parents about school and perhaps a celebratory dinner at Sorrento's Pizzeria. My parents knew nothing about my daily assignments or quiz scores, but they knew I was a reasonably intelligent kid who would find my way, and they kept most of their focus on molding me as a good human being.

Now thanks to apps like Grade Tracker, I'm not the only parent to be notified when their kid doesn't turn in their Spanish homework. Students, too, can see their grade change for the better or worse in real time. It's the embodiment of the digital clock, and it changes the equation from the big-picture, long-term issues (am I raising a good human being?) to one of instant reactions (why didn't my kid do better on that math quiz?).

Consider, too, the experiences of kids like my daughters, Ruby and Eliana, who, in addition to getting their grades in real time, are also getting their social approval that way. We've all seen teenagers glued to their phones, waiting for the next "ding" to alert them that they've been tagged in someone's photo, or that someone has "liked" their latest post. What is that doing to their brains and the quality of their thoughts and feelings? If you think about the brain as a spotlight, that spotlight is only looking three or four feet around. There's an old

Hindu parable you may have heard about a mystic searching for his key on the ground. When someone stops to help him look, that person asks where exactly he dropped it. "In my own house," says the mystic. "Then why are you looking here?" the helper asks. The mystic then explains, "There's more light here."[4] Similarly, that teenager doesn't think about who they are or who they want to be—they're just looking at where the light's shining. They don't talk to the friend in need sitting next to them because that friend on TikTok has posted a sad-face emoji. They're apt to forget what an *actual* sad face looks like, and how to read it. And their brains become so addicted to the dopamine rush that "ding!" offers them that it takes more and more to satisfy them.[5] The brain is in a perpetual stance of awaiting the next hit.

Our ancestors who lived in agrarian societies wouldn't know what to make of us. Their whole concept of time—which midwife Nancy Bardacke calls "horticultural time"—was dependent on seasons and sunrises. It wasn't until the Industrial Age that societies were introduced to "machine time," which is precise, predictable, and efficient. Those ancestors had watches to set and trains to catch. Then came our grandparents, who learned to measure time differently yet again—in terms of a consumer's attention span. It was just in the last century that we discovered the specific mechanisms for manipulating the human mind and amplifying its short-term tendencies for self-serving purposes.

In the 1950s, post-war America was poised for a time of growth and prosperity, save for a problem: Those returning GIs and their spouses were all children of the Great Depression, who had come of age during wartime. Their lives thus far had taught them to conserve, not splurge. A guy named Edward Bernays exploded on the scene just as these GIs were returning from Europe. Called the "father of public relations," he believed that human beings weren't all that rational, and could be easily manipulated if you knew what you were doing. (Interestingly, he was also a nephew of Sigmund Freud.) Using crowd psychology and propaganda as early as the 1920s, he realized how to prey on our most base instincts—like our needs for belonging and safety in numbers—and use that to stoke demand for clients like tobacco companies and Dixie cups. All the cool kids smoked, and the only safe way to prevent the spread of germs was to use disposable cups. Bernays crafted campaigns that would prey on these needs, in order to encourage us to make split-second impulse buys.

Madison Avenue used the psychology touted by Bernays to convince the GI and his wife that they were not in fact irresponsible if they bought a Cadillac, or a television set (that would, incidentally, bring about more access to advertising and mental distractions). In fact, it was their patriotic duty to use their purchasing power to buy, and to buy American. What is particularly striking about this approach isn't just that it played on our species' collective love of short-term pleasure, it also touched on our evolutionary need to belong. In other words, just as our ancestors wanted to be sheltered in the cave at night with the rest of the tribe, we felt we *needed* to buy these Cadillacs to feel accepted and therefore safe. The consumer capitalism that resulted preys on our base need for security by stoking demand for a bunch of stuff, and a lifestyle, we—and the planet—don't need.

The painful thing about the consumer culture of the last century is that it's hard to recognize our participation in the machine. That's part of the design: Consumer capitalism not only thrives on our disconnection, it actually depends on it. Every time you order a hamburger from a drive-thru, the company that is selling it to you doesn't also sell you the story of the cow, or the meat-packing factory, or the cramped living conditions of the folks who work there. If it did, you might not buy that burger. Instead, the company's selling you a story of a really hungry, attractive person who wants to bite into a delicious, affordable juicy burger while kicking back with friends all living their best life. And because companies have a mandate for growth, their goal is to sell more products in more locations and to invest more in making you believe that you actually want them.

As we already know, this game of Hungry Hungry Hippo we're playing is problematic. When it comes to physical consumption, we simply don't have room or resources for all the stuff we're producing. It took two hundred thousand years for our population to reach one billion, and only two hundred years to reach seven billion.[6] That kind of growth might be all well and good if Earth itself was ever expanding, but it's not. By adding all that we are, we are defying the bounds of physics. There's a certain amount of resources that we can take out each year and still regenerate it—but we usually "run out" by midsummer. Any kid with a bank account can see the problem: We are taking out more than we put back in. And that's largely because we're so focused on the short term that we're not asking basic questions about what it is we *really* want, what our endgame is.

How to Change Our Short-Term Minds

When I was in middle school, our school had this gardener who, my friends and I would all joke, must have always come to work directly from the bar. You could see the lawn mower tracks over the football and soccer field, and they were never, ever straight. He mowed that lawn with complete abandon. Was he listening to music and dancing along on his mower? Was he messing with us? Was he leaving some sort of symbol or signal for aliens in the patterns he created? The same was true for his weeding. He would pull weeds in one spot only to completely ignore another.

Fast-forward about twenty years, and I had the chance to study garden design with a revered Japanese master gardener from the famous Golden Temple in Kyoto. He had traveled to San Diego to teach, and my classmates and I were helping him build a tea garden and larger garden complex in San Diego's famed Balboa Park. As he explained what we were going to do—which involved a bridge and a faux river made of stones—I looked around for the machinery I presumed we'd use and wondered if I could call dibs on the Bobcat. But he informed us that we would be doing it all using six-hundred-year-old techniques; our primary tools would be our hands. For hours, my job was to place stones in such a way that they would represent rippling, flowing water. I contemplated each and every placement of each and every four-inch stone. When heavy, unrelenting rain began to fall—a rarity in San Diego—I guessed that we would stop and pick up our work the next day. Instead, he asked us to gather and watch the water as it pooled and flowed, so we would understand the why and how of what we were doing.

The difference between these two gardeners in my life is pretty clear: My middle school gardener was unfocused and unintentional; the Kyoto master gardener was deliberate about every single action. The garden, I've always thought, is a good metaphor for the brain. We get to choose what kind of gardeners of our body's most complex organ we want to be. We can let the lawn grow willy-nilly, or we can recognize the difference between a weed and a flower, and diligently, intentionally, get rid of the former. We can drive the mower haphazardly, or we can prune away the excess stuff that keeps us from growing and bearing healthy fruit. If we want a brain that thinks Long-path, we're going to need to weed and fertilize the gardens of our brains pretty intentionally.

Step 1 is paying attention. As every self-help guru, rabbi, minister, or yoga teacher has already told you, notice what's happening before letting your more uninformed habits take hold. If you're constantly checking your email or stuffing your face with junk food, for instance, how is your mood? How is it affecting your connection with others? Is it getting you closer to being a better, more evolved human who will spread better, more evolved human-ness? Probably not.

Step 2 is believing we can do better. While there are immense capacities for both human good and evil, there is growing evidence that we are more capable of good than we give ourselves credit for. Whereas we used to think all of the growth and changes to our brains happened before adulthood, now we know that brains change all the time—and we can have a hand in changing them to what we want them to look like. Carol Dweck's research on the growth mindset, which comes from cutting-edge neuroscience work about neuroplasticity in the brain, is the most popular understanding of this. Basically, Dweck taught us that instead of thinking, "I'm not good at math," we should think, "I'm not good at math *yet*." When we adopt the latter mindset, we are a good part of the way toward actually being good at math.[7] And the same goes for our humanity. We are not a peaceful and loving species who care about future generations, *yet*. But thinking that we can be puts us well on our way to *actually being* better.

Step 3 We can then move on to cultivating our Longpathian selves, en masse. Because in addition to deciding we *can* be humans who think about the far-off future, we should probably be more proactive about making it happen.

LET'S PRACTICE OUR ABCs. **We'll start with Awareness.** Think about how your typical day begins. Was your sleep interrupted by an alarm? Did you check your phone for notifications or messages before even getting out of bed? How many people or tasks did you think about while you were brushing your teeth or taking a shower? How many family feuds did you have to moderate before breakfast? Do you remember what your breakfast tasted like? Does coffee count as breakfast? Do you have your morning schedule broken down to the exact nanosecond that you have to be out the door? Did your morning make you feel spacious or tight? Did you feel capable of being present with those around you or were you barely keeping one foot in front of the other? See how a hyper-focus on short-term results might make it hard to think about far futures?

Okay. Let's move on to Belief. This one's simple. Are you willing to imagine a morning that is not rush, rush, rush? Are you willing to believe that the pace of life can slow down without life leaving you behind? Are you willing to entertain the idea that you are more than the sum of your clicks? Are you willing to acknowledge that it might be a good thing to consider how Manic Mornings may be impacting your experience of being human? Yes? Great! Let's try to Cultivate a different reality. Perhaps you're already in a position where your employer offers a flexible schedule or remote work option. What shifts in your daily habits would allow you to ease into your day and make you feel like you are acting with more intention? How might you integrate a long-term goal into your routine? If you don't have much choice around your schedule, can you identify one or two attention thieves in your life and find a work-around to reclaim your time? Would applying parental controls to your social media accounts free up ten minutes to connect with a real, live human being? Would a house rule about laying out clothes in the evening reduce choice anxiety and stress in the morning? What morning habits can you model today that future generations will thank you for?

A Longpath mindset requires us to strengthen a particular set of competencies, including the use of our prosocial emotions such as empathy, gratitude, and awe. Strengthening these "muscles" allows us to think and feel more deeply about the past, present, and future, to understand our place in time, and to care for others who have not yet been born. There are many great scientific minds researching how to develop prosocial emotions. Foremost among them is Martin Seligman, considered the father of positive psychology. He has long argued that instead of identifying all the ways people are miserable and fixing them, let's identify what makes people strong and find ways to emphasize and build on those traits. Psychology shouldn't just be about remediating problems, he says, but encouraging practices that make us better.

Researchers such as David DeSteno of Northeastern's Social Emotions Group and Jamil Zaki, director of Stanford's Social Neuroscience Lab, take the mantle from here, showing us that prosocial emotions are skills that can be built. "These emotions have been used as technologies by spiritual traditions for thousands of years to foster virtue (which usually requires a future orientation) as opposed to vice (which is usually characterized by a desire for immediate pleasure)," said DeSteno. "And now science is showing that these emotions—for which there exist innate capacities—actually alter our behavior."[8] DeSteno's lab has shown that intentionally paying attention through meditation practice can foster compassion and that expressing gratitude can make us less likely to consume finite resources.[9] And as Zaki says of empathy, "When we practice engaging over and over again, we build an empathy that is bigger, broader, more muscular." In one empathy study, for instance, there was a significant gap between women and men in their ability to accurately judge what other people were feeling (guess which gender did better?). But that gap was eliminated when the study participants were told they'd be paid for their accuracy. This isn't about picking on men (remember, for hundreds of years, our entire culture has devalued the feminine), but to show how malleable we are. "If we have a reason to practice empathy," Zaki said, "we do, and we get better in the process."[11] What's more, if we're *told* that our empathy is something that can be grown, that it's within our power to build these more empathic brain connections, we are more likely to do so.[12]

As we all do this, prosocial tendencies become a cultural default that self-replicates, and we nurture brains that do not immediately jump to short-termism. Instead, we receive powerful cues from other people and our environments that suggest a benefit to delaying our immediate gratification—a system override. The base instincts will still be there, of course. Remember, we still resemble our ancient selves. But we can recognize they're there, say hello, and then choose to act differently, and to alter the story for whoever comes next. We can be more intentional about selecting what it takes to be a stellar human being, and then garden for *that*. (And just like a garden, the plans can change, needs evolve, and the work is never really done.) In being more proactive, we move from trying to sustain what was to recognizing our innate power to create and regenerate, helping us become better than we were before. We pass that along to the next generation, and they in turn pass it on. In essence, we ensure the next generation starts out on a higher terrace.

The Longpath Pillars

I've resisted calling short-termism "Enemy #1," because, again, it has served us well in the past. Now, however, as we weather a stormy Intertidal that warns of environmental, social, and economic collapse, we have to put short-termism firmly on the sideline. Short-termism causes us to be reactionary and individual-minded when what will get us through this time is thinking expansively and collectively. But we need a process to replace it—which is where Longpath comes in.

Longpath has two critical pillars that are designed to combat the forces of short-termism, and to help you "garden" a brain that brings in a much bigger picture with every decision, even when those decisions lie deep beneath the surface of your consciousness. Those pillars are:

Transgenerational Empathy: A continual awareness of your place in a chain of being, wherein you reckon with your inherited history, find alignment in and with the present, and make adjustments to improve the future.

Futures Thinking and Telos: An expansive capacity to think about many different types of futures and an invitation to imagine the future you want.

These pillars teach you to think bigger than the here and now. Used together, they create a process that helps us become great ancestors for future generations. And just as we become more empathetic simply by knowing it's a buildable skill, you are already more apt to live Longpath in your life just by knowing it, too, is a buildable skill. (See what I did there?) You are more likely to talk about Longpath with a friend or to drop it into a conversation, further cementing its hold.

Longpath holds these pillars within a simple word you can write down on calendars, chalkboards, and Post-it notes, or whisper under your breath, centering you and reminding you what to do next and why. It's an invitation to see how your day changes. To notice how your neurons fire just a little differently. Then to do it again the next day.

I use Longpath daily—*hourly*—in my life. I use it in decisions I make about how to spend my time, how to spend my money, how to talk to myself, and how to be with others around me. It doesn't make my life perfect, but it does make it intentional. It gives me pause to think, What is the point of this? Why is it here, and what does it have to do with the future I want to create?

Yes, that seems heady for the simple decisions that make up daily life. But it reverberates outward, to the CEO who has Longpath written on a whiteboard for a weekly budget meeting *and* at her corporate leadership retreat. And indeed, I've used Longpath to help some of the biggest organizations in the world make decisions. Longpath reverberates outward from there to a society that two hundred years from now might find concepts like justice wholly unnecessary, because why *wouldn't* we all be fair and just to one another?

You are likely (hopefully?) already starting to live Longpath, just from having read these first chapters. Now is where the work goes even deeper, from the theoretical to the individual, from the civilizational to the personal.

The next chapter challenges you to consider where you fit within the bigger picture—and part of doing so means recognizing not just that we're looking forward, but that it's just as important to think (and *feel*) back. Way, way back.

Looking Backward, Inward, and Forward

We are the past. We are the result of many thousands and millions of years. We are the result of racial, accumulated experience and knowledge. We are the result of tradition and influence. We are, deep down, the residue of everything involved in the past. That is the deep, hidden, secret, unexposed part of our mind.[1]

—J. KRISHNAMURTI

Recently I came across a fifty-year-old collage painting of market stalls and street life my mom created when she lived in Mexico, a canvas filled with vibrant colors and shapes. The back of the painting was covered with newspapers documenting the triumphs and tragedies of Mexico City on a day in 1970. The pairing made sense. For my mom, life was always about context. When we would wander through art galleries during my childhood, she pointed out the artists' use of perspective, light, and shapes, but she also posed questions—mostly unanswerable—about the artists' inner and outer worlds. "What do you think the artist was thinking when they created this?" Or "What do you think was going on—and had gone on—in their life? Their society?" You couldn't look at any one person or thing without considering the world around it, the world that shaped it. A desire for context, a craving to understand how her San Francisco Bay Area upbringing fit into a larger picture, was the reason she'd left the United States to study in Mexico in the first place. In fact, it was her teacher, the futurist Buckminster Fuller, who recommended she expand her aesthetic horizons beyond classic Western notions.

My mom's influence shows up not just in the way I look at

art, but in how I look at everything. If I read an article about a horrible act by some politician, I can see how the act is indisputably horrible. And I also think about the context: What made them act that way? What was their upbringing like? What forces were at play in *their* parents' upbringing? Their grandparents'? I'm not trying to excuse the action, but to understand it. We all too often start and stop the blame based on that single individual's actions—it's a life span bias that gets in our way of seeing both the underlying causes of actions and possible positive ways forward. Nothing is ever clear-cut, nothing is ever completely binary. In this way, I bring my mom with me in the very way I think about the world, and in how I move through it.

My dad is also with me in everything I do. When I was young, our family would take occasional daylong Amtrak train rides from Walnut Creek up to the western Sierra Mountains through steep canyons to our ultimate vacation destination—Reno! I distinctly remember overhearing my parents talk on the first trip, and my dad saying with wonder, "You know, the last time I was in a really snowy canyon like this, I had a machine gun. I didn't know where my next meal was coming from. And we didn't know which bend in the trail would have Nazis hiding behind it. When I went to bed, I'd sleep with my gun in my hand, the safety off. I didn't know how I would wake up—would it be from the sun? Or from a German flashlight? Or would I wake up at all? Now here I am, drinking coffee, while my three kids are looking out at the snow-covered trees drinking hot chocolate and coloring." The way he said it, it was like science fiction to him; it was so surreal that he had been *there,* and now he was *here.* At the heart of this memory is my dad's unbending sense of awe, even after everything he had been through and his conviction—passed on to me—that really anything is possible. Although we obviously have limitations, we also have agency. As with my mom's, my father's beliefs, too, inform my work at Longpath Labs every single day. It's what I think of when I read the latest analysis of how we are steering the ship of humanity into an iceberg, and think, yeah, but what if we turned the ship? And how might we turn that ship?

Contemplation of your parents' experiences illustrates a central Longpath pillar: Transgenerational Empathy. Transgenerational Empathy encourages you to be continually aware of your place in a chain of being. You explore the needs, choices, and feelings of those who came before you—the first link in the chain toward becoming great ancestors. The second link involves examining your own self-actualization, having self-empathy within a transgenerational context. The third link requires you to explore the needs and desires of humans living generations from now, Transgenerational Empathy for the future. Examining all of these links together is how you traverse the long path, how you begin to understand your role in a massive, millennia-long production. It is how you can future better, and start to cultivate a Longpath mindset.

IN THE BOOK'S OPENING epigraph, I shared the story of Choni, who came across a man planting a carob tree, though he knew he wouldn't live to see it provide shade, but planted it because his ancestors had planted one for him. What are the carob trees that have been planted for you?

Take a few minutes to consider how your experiences today have been shaped by the choices—both external and internal—of previous generations, and how they made them. What if you imagine the experiences of the next generation to come? How would they—your future descendants—answer that question about you? Does it align with what you would want them to know about your life? What if you asked these questions of yourself every day—multiple times a day? What if you asked, "What would my grandfather have thought? How is that affecting my view of the world? How will my great-grandchildren feel about this?" Perhaps you're considering taking a job with a high salary, but the company culture is supposedly terrible, the hours long, the sense of meaning in the work null. You imagine your forebears would have laughed that you even had to pause. Providing for the family was everything to them. Is that value still with you, unnoticed? How do you want your great-grandchildren to feel about taking such a job? Now, what if you didn't just think it, but you could feel it? Using that information—both the logical and the emotional—to guide your choices is one of the fundamentals of Long-path.

In Western culture, at least, we've typically stuck to a more limited framework to guide our choices. My parents raised me on the wisdom of well-known philosophers like Plato, Aristotle, Socrates, Nietzsche, and Kant. And these guys are great and all, but they did one thing that, as I look at it now, not only bums me out, but makes me question so much of how we think about the meaning of life. They all took the single human life span, from birth to death, as their unit of measurement for what it meant to be virtuous and good.

We can't think about the problems facing our world, like food security or climate change, or even the problems facing our families, like emotional well-being, and limit our thinking to the single life span as the unit of measurement. When we do, we fall into "lifespan bias." With a Longpath lens, we think longer and, importantly, in both directions. We think about the past—our mothers' experiences and our great-great-great-

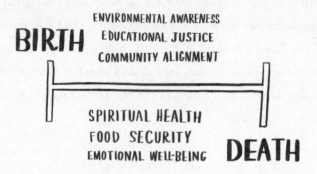

grandmothers'—and the future—our children's, nieces', and nephews', as well as their great-great-great-grandchildren's, grandnieces', and grandnephews'.

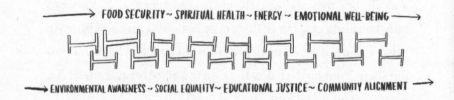

Transgenerational Empathy is an antidote to short-termism because it helps us prioritize long-term objectives over short-term gains. It is a reminder that you are a link in the chain of being—that a lot happened before you came on the scene, and a lot will happen after you leave it. And so much of what happens after you leave depends on what you do, think, and feel while you do the little song and dance called "my life."

Empathy for Our Ancestors

The great force of history comes from the fact that we carry
it within us, are unconsciously controlled by it in many
ways, and history is literally present in all that we do.

—JAMES BALDWIN

I am acutely aware of my own inheritance on some days,
and how some of my reflexes are related to my father's past. My
wife, Sharon, and I took a marathon shopping trip to Trader
Joe's, for instance, and as we took our two full carts out to the
car, she pointed out that it would take some time to unload everything at home. "I'll take the bags with the freezer stuff down
to the basement," I said. Sharon had helped the checker bag
everything while I was busy throwing more stuff we probably
didn't need into the cart, and she pointed out that she hadn't
separated all the freezer items into bags separate from pantry
items. For some reason, this triggered me, and I snapped at her.

"I'm not an expert bagger!" she reminded me. "What's
going on with you?"

I wisely kept my mouth shut while I considered why it was that I was so triggered. What was going through my head when I snapped? I'd been thinking of Sharon: *You should know the right thing to do. You should always know. You're not just a wife, but you're a mom, and you should know.* I'm not saying these were fair thoughts—just that they were my subconscious thoughts.

I could trace them easily to my dad, who would often get angry with my mom for the same kind of stupid reasons. I wondered why he'd done that. (Per my mom's influence on me, there always had to be a why.) I thought of his relationships with the women in his life. He had always talked about his own mother glowingly. But I'd long suspected that deep down inside, he was angry with her—for not doing the right thing when the Holocaust was starting, for not leaving, for not somehow saving herself—which would have been impossible. She didn't know the right thing to do, and I believe he always felt abandoned and therefore angry as a result.

In "The Case of TJ's Frozen Goods," I was able to put two and two together pretty quickly. But other times the ways I carry my ancestral history are much more subconscious. It's like how when you first put pants on in the morning, you feel the constriction of the waistband. But then, unless the pants are way too tight, you stop feeling them. That's because at the base of your brain, there's this thing called the RAS, the reticular activating system, which filters out stimuli and signals that the sensation, in this case your waistband, is not necessary to be aware of right now. We wouldn't be able to productively go on with our day if our brains were focused on our pants all the time. But that doesn't mean we're not wearing them, or that they don't impact the way we move about. Sometimes they are just filtered out for the sake of expediency. But we wear our history the same way, whether that history is good, or whether it's bad. And sometimes it really is very bad.

Our ability to practice Transgenerational Empathy is vulnerable around trauma, whether our ancestors were the perpetrators or recipients, and this is true on a personal and societal scale. When the past is unconscionable or even just uncomfortable, even when it is a past from before we were born, we have a tendency to either keep our eyes trained forward ("The past doesn't matter—'To Infinity and Beyond!'"), or to grow defensive ("It's not like I'm the one who did those horrible things."). But in doing either, we fail to learn from the past, or to recognize that, just like that waistband of those pants, we're still wearing it every single day of our lives. Not acknowledging the profound influence the past has on our current ways of being— as individuals and as a society—is like applying duct tape to a broken water pipe. Yes, it might hold for the short term, but eventually, it will burst through, and the resulting flood will be worse than we could ever imagine.

That's why empathy for the past has everything to do with the future. Transgenerational Empathy allows you to see what made you, you. It shows you the baggage you brought—or rather inherited—into the space of your life. It helps you put the past in its proper place, so that you recognize that how much of what you *think* you want has come from others. This knowledge causes you to think differently . . . it enables you to think Longpath.

The empathy piece of Transgenerational Empathy is what allows us to learn from the past and take it with us in all the best ways. Empathy is different from compassion. Empathy is the ability to get beyond your ego and imagine how someone else feels. That doesn't mean you would feel that way, too, or that you think they're right to feel that way, just that you can imagine it.

If empathy for your forebears is difficult, imagine how, in 2150, your great-great-grandchildren will view *your* life. Perhaps there will be some technology that allows humans to read the thoughts of animals, and our descendants will look at our decisions to eat meat as barbaric. And they will most definitely look at the way we ignored climate change and be enraged, or at the very least mystified. While we can and should let these possibilities guide us to better decisions now, we also have the benefit of being here now. We're trying to do the best we can with what we know, and we have to give our ancestors that same benefit of the doubt.

Let me be clear that having empathy for our ancestors doesn't mean letting anyone off the hook. Not us, and especially not our ancestors who may have committed atrocities. We're not placating. We're recognizing that they operated in a psychological and social environment that was different from ours, and that no one has a monopoly on the perfected status of anything. Our ancestors, too, were raised by links on the chain going back centuries. Empathy for our ancestors requires humility and taking a nuanced approach, even as we see them clearly. We learn nothing when we write them off, least of all an understanding of how their actions *then* impact ours *today*.

Bringing the past to light can help us to disrupt the entrenched patterns of suffering on individual and societal scales. In South Africa, a Truth and Reconciliation Commission was established after apartheid to allow the victims of human rights abuses to tell their stories and to permit the perpetrators of those abuses to assume responsibility for their actions and request pardon. While not perfect, the commission has been deemed largely successful in the country's ability to move forward in a manner based on restoration, not reprisal. The truth and reconciliation process involves honesty, an opportunity to mourn, to forgive, and to heal. Different societies have grappled with this concept in their own ways. In Budapest, Memento Park houses statues from the darkest days of the communist era, where visitors can consider the past without glorifying it. As travel writer Cameron Hewitt points out, "While it's possible that a few nostalgic old-timers come here to get misty-eyed about the 'good old days' of communism, it's clear to me that the vast majority of visitors are here to ogle these monstrosities, to learn about the era they represent . . . and to take a 'victory lap' around the now-pitiful remains of a failed empire. For those seeking historical context, archival photographs show the statues *in situ*. Because, obviously, you don't need to keep a symbol of oppression in a prominent place just to ensure that it's remembered."[2]

And then there's Germany. Lawyer, activist, and founder of the Equal Justice Initiative, Bryan Stevenson, has said that the reason he's able to visit Berlin is that Germans very publicly recognize the horrors of the Holocaust, with plaques on houses where Jewish families lived and a prominent memorial museum. "If no one acknowledged it, if no one talked about it," he said, "it wouldn't matter how nice people were in the moment—I couldn't trust a society that did something that horrific and refused to acknowledge the horror of it. . . ." If we're not aware of the "pasts" we're wearing, we're not just blind to dangers of it happening again; we perpetuate the pain by disavowing the loss.

Some governments lead efforts to reconcile with the past, which is great, but we don't have to rely on government to do this work. If enough individuals talk about their shared past, if enough people are attuned to the needs of integrating those pasts and learning from them, it can become a cultural zeitgeist.

As an example, Stevenson's Equal Justice Initiative is one

of the leaders in this effort to reckon with America's past. It hosts a project where participants can take a jar, a gardening implement, and information about a lynching site and collect soil from the site as a way to honor and remember the victims. When one participant, who was Black, did this on the side of the road in west Alabama, she noticed—with some trepidation—a truck slow down, and then pull to a stop, nearby. A big white guy got out and asked her what she was doing, and she said, "This is where a Black man was lynched in 1937, and I'm going to honor his life."

As Stevenson tells it, "And she said she got nervous so she started digging real fast, and the man just stood there. And then she said the man said, 'Does that paper talk about the lynching?' She said, 'It does.' And then he said, 'Can I read it?' She said yes. She gave the man the paper and she kept digging. And the man read the paper, and then he put it down. And then he shocked her when he said, 'Excuse me, but would it be okay if I helped you?' She said yes, and then the man got down on his knees. She offered him the implement to dig the soil, and he said, 'No, no, no, no. You use that. I'll just use my hands.' She said that this man started throwing his hands into the soil with such force and commitment and picking up the soil and putting it in the jar. She said his hands were black with the soil. There was something about the way he just gave it his all that moved her. She started crying, and the man stopped and said,

'Oh, I'm so sorry I'm upsetting you.' 'No, no, no, you're blessing me,' she said. She kept digging with her implement and he kept digging with his hands, and they were getting near the top of the jar and she looked over at him and she could see his shoulder shaking. Then she saw tears running down his face, and she stopped. She said, 'Are you okay?' and he said, 'No, ma'am. I just, I'm just so worried that it might have been my grandfather that participated in lynching this man.' " [3]

By digging this soil together, they were able to collectively connect with the trauma and pain of the past in a way that acknowledged its presence in their life today—even from wildly disparate lived experiences. The act didn't gloss over the past or lead to a kumbaya moment, but, hopefully, it did play a role in building a foundation for reconciliation (not forgetting!) that would allow them both to move forward to building better tomorrows.

The story of this soil is vivid, just as lynching is a dramatic example of the sins of our fathers. Transgenerational Empathy isn't always this clear, this overt—sometimes it's an entirely internal process, like the one I went through after I snapped at Sharon about the frozen foods. But it is a journey we all must take—individually and collectively—if we are to Longpath. In order to think of the future, you have to connect with where it all started.

FIND A ROOM THAT offers some privacy, where you feel safe, and stand in front of a mirror (preferably full-length). When you are ready, remove your clothing. This is not a self-shame exercise or anything weird, so do your best to reserve any judgment that may come up. Start by looking at the skin on your stomach. Now move your attention to just your belly button. There are roughly four million cells in just the one square inch skin surrounding this area. Many years ago, this spot was a lifeline for you while you gestated in your mother's womb—in the exact same way that humans have been nourished for millennia and pre-humans for millennia before them. And even before that, the wee little egg that was fertilized and eventually became you? It was created when your mother was a fetus being carried by your grandmother a generation ago. Let that sink in.

Now here you are, in all your majesty, evolved to the point where you are standing in a room in your home. That body in the mirror is you and the billions of sapiens that came before you—from the shape of your feet (built for walking across the desolate savanna for hours a day) to the most amazing organ ever to have existed on planet Earth—your brain. Your body is telling a biological story, and it is humbling and awesome, with the emphasis on the awe.

Gaze at your feet, knees, hips, hands, shoulders, face, eyes. All evolved to their current configuration based on those who came before you. In your form, you see your super-ancient relatives who used their muscular torsos to hunt, and you also see your sweet Grandma Rosie in the shape of your smile. When you reach to turn off the lights at night, you're using the same muscular reflexes that every ancestor who came before you did. And your fear of the dark might be part of your lineage, too. This body of yours is inherited, and so are the lived experiences of your ancestors. For every physical trait that you see, there are thousands upon thousands of cultural, behavioral, and environmental legacies that you carry.

Now, slowly raise your right hand and place it over your heart, and let the left hand softly rest over your belly. Feel the rise and fall of your chest and stomach as you breathe in and out, and notice the steady pulse of your heart beating. Ask yourself:

What of my ancestral inheritance do I want to take with me?

What do I want to leave behind?

Take a moment to jot down your responses and keep this mirror experience with you as you make decisions in your life—both big and small.

Empathy for Self

Joseph Campbell wrote, "For we travel—each—in two worlds: An inwards of our own awareness, and an outwards of participation in the history of our time and place." For Longpath to have a grip, these two worlds must work together. We cannot be good descendants or great ancestors if we are not living our lives fully and authentically. And so the Empathy for Self portion of Transgenerational Empathy is about living an *aligned* life. Two tools that can help with such alignment are 1) a practice of self-compassion and 2) an acknowledgment of the finite nature of our lives and the potentially infinite nature of our legacies.

Self-compassion is a willingness to take a kind and forgiving attitude toward our foibles and missteps, while still doing the work to make amends. It is self-compassion that allows us to learn from our mistakes and to move forward, to *act*, better. Consider "The Case of TJ's Frozen Goods" from earlier in this chapter. I could not have admitted my fault in snapping at Sharon if I hadn't also been willing to give myself a break.

Jamil Zaki, from Stanford's Social Neuroscience Lab, has studied self-compassion extensively, and he says that its lack in our lives hobbles us—it causes us to become rigid during conflict, and it prevents us from compromising when we disagree.[4] Imagine a high schooler who blows a big test because, though she had the best of intentions to study the night before, she got on TikTok instead and ended up staying up much too late. When she learns her grade, she internalizes some pretty terrible thoughts: *I'm so dumb, of course I got a bad grade. I'm an irresponsible idiot.* When her parents inquire about her grade, her sense of shame puts her in a rigid, defensive position, and she comes out swinging. If this girl had self-compassion, however, her internal dialogue would be different: *I mean well, I try, and sometimes I mess up. Getting on TikTok that night wasn't my best decision, but I also was feeling buried and needed a release. But it's okay. I'm going to own up to this mistake but move past it. Maybe I'll ask if there are extra-credit opportunities.*

Companies, communities, and entire societies benefit from committing to self-compassion work. It's what allows them to keep from getting stuck in shame of past failures—and sometimes it is a wise PR move. You may remember that Starbucks came under fire in 2018 when a barista in Philadelphia, for no justifiable reason, called the police on two Black men in the store. Rather than adopt a defensive posture ("That was just one barista out of thousands!"), Starbucks was able to say (and I'm paraphrasing), *This feels awful. Even good companies screw up sometimes. We want to do better.* They closed eight thousand stores for an afternoon in order to offer anti-bias training to their employees.

NASA has similarly committed to learning from mistakes—which would not be possible if they were hung up on denying them or excusing them. They have a "Pause and Learn Process," wherein teammates regularly check in about what works and what doesn't. No good or bad consequences come from these meetings—the emphasis is on honesty and a spirit of moving forward better. If people know that bad consequences come from reviewing what happened, they are less likely to admit what they did, or to push back defensively when confronted. No one learns anything. On the flip side, "Pause and Learn" offers truth, reconciliation, and recommitment to what everyone is there for in the first place. And in NASA's case, that goal is literally reaching space. Another moniker for the same essential process is the after-action review, an exercise of self-awareness and learning from mistakes that's been adopted by the Army and organizations like Shell and Harley-Davidson.

LET'S TRY OUR OWN Pause, Learn—and Realign—process using some loving-kindness techniques toward ourselves. Take a moment and bring to mind an experience that you wish had gone better. You can start small or go big—just remember that we're not here to cause any more harm to ourselves or others. Gently take a breath and see if you can trace your choices and responses back to a distinct feeling or sensation in your body that preceded the turning point in your scenario. Stay with that feeling for a little while. Is there anything else that is coming up for you? Is there an emotion beneath the emotion or thoughts or memories that are arising? Are there other times in your life that you felt the same way? Okay, great job. Now let's take another deep breath, maybe two breaths, and ask ourselves, "How do I wish I (or we) had felt after this experience? What could I (or we) have done better?" I'm betting that this line of questioning feels much better than the one before. Hold on to that warm sensation for a little while. When you're ready, let's practice some self-compassion. Repeat to yourself:

I am a perfectly imperfect human being who is learning.
I am a learning human being who is aspiring to apply what I have learned.

I am an aspiring human being who is healing my unhealthy habits.

I am a healing human being who is still fallible.

I am a fallible human being who is working hard to align my actions with my values.

You may come up with your own phrases over time; the words should feel authentic to you. The main idea is that we can draw wisdom from our experiences and lay down all of the difficult emotions that make it hard for us to move on or to even examine ourselves in the first place. Consider writing down a few notes about your experience doing this exercise, including ways that you would handle a similar scenario in the future. You may want to circle the "desired feeling" in your notes and use that word as an anchor for you during difficult situations.

There's a lot of learning and realignment for us to do during our life spans and a finite amount of time to do it all. Living an aligned life comes with an acceptance that inevitably, one day, we won't be alive, and this fact gives everything we do in our life meaning. This is probably where you roll your eyes and say, "Yeah, I've heard the Tim McGraw song—live like you're dying. Skydiving and Rocky Mountain climbing and all that. Live every day as if it will be your last. Seize the day. Got it." Hallmark cards and country music songs aside, most of us are still not living that way. It's not that we need to take more risks or eat dessert first, and we certainly don't want to be more short-term oriented than we already are. Rather, we want to acknowledge death so we can live in alignment with what we care about, so that the impact of our life reverberates in space and, most important, in time. You Only Live Once (YOLO) changes to Your Life Is Bigger Than You (not as cool an acronym, admittedly).

Human beings are unique in that we don't *have* to be engaged in a near-death situation to understand that death is coming for all of us, and that it could come at any time. This is frightening knowledge to live with. As Ernest Becker wrote in his Pulitzer Prize–winning *The Denial of Death*, "Man is literally split in two: he has an awareness of his own splendid uniqueness in that he sticks out of nature with a towering majesty, and yet he goes back into the ground a few feet in order blindly and dumbly to rot and disappear forever. It is a terrifying dilemma to be in and to have to live with."[5]

The most common response to our fear of death is denial—or, at least, avoidance. We shove thoughts of death under the rug. Sure, our impending death is an elephant, but our rug is really big—it's more like a wall-to-wall carpet, really. And if the elephant creeps out, we'll just get a bigger carpet, or upgrade to shag, never mind how impractical it is. Denial is why so many people don't fill out a power of attorney or create a will—this is true even for many who suffer from a terminal illness. It's why people will put off visiting an aging or dying relative—it's just too uncomfortable. The rug isn't stretchy enough for that encounter. This denial inclination explains why, though 80 percent of Americans want to die at home, only 20 percent of us do. It explains why clinicians ask about their terminal patients' goals for the last phase of their lives less than *one-third* of the time. Even the doctors don't want to talk about it![6]

On the flip side, those who work in jobs that encounter death speak of the great sense of purpose they feel every day, their sense of alignment. Anthony Back, who founded the Palliative Care Center of Excellence, talks about the courage and frankness of terminal patients who openly face their impending death, making intentional and meaningful plans for their last days. "What I've concluded," he said, "is that there is something enlivening about facing one's own mortality and vulnerability."[7] Laura Carstensen, a psychologist and the director of the Stanford Center on Longevity, found something similar when she looked into why older people reported less stress, worry, anger, and psychological distress than younger people. She found that as their time on earth grew shorter, their goals grew deeper and their emotional lives grew richer, including their capacity to forgive and reconcile with themselves and with others.[8]

We don't have to be older, or be sick, to contemplate our deaths and thereby live fuller lives. It can be something we do as a matter of course in the day-to-day. For instance, I was once asked to consult with an everyone-is-talking-about-him TV director who was feeling "stuck" as he embarked on a big, ambitious project. I said, "In the 2080s, someone is sitting down and opening their morning newspaper. They're reading your obituary, and the first paragraph talks about your illustrious directing career. The second is all about what a great guy you were to friends and family. The third paragraph is about *this* project. What is it about this project that makes it deserve to be the third paragraph of your obituary?" His eyes got big, and I swear I could see the alignment happening. We spent the rest of the meeting focusing on the themes and concepts that were most important to his view of the world—concepts that had been in the project all along, but that he had not voiced or thought to emphasize. Like most of us, this director had been in the stupor of the present, but questions of death broke him out. To tap into the Longpath mindset we must confront and reconcile with what I believe is one of the biggest roadblocks to our taking actions on behalf of future generations—our death. To do this we must all engage with this most difficult of mental time travel—to the time after you.

CHOOSE A SIGNIFICANT VENTURE or effort in your life, something that takes a great deal of your time and energy. It could be your work, a volunteer project you've taken on, or an event you're organizing. Now, consider that project within a eulogy context. Does it belong in your eulogy? Is it the third paragraph? If so, write it. Or is it a line thrown in somewhere near the bottom? Or is it something you wouldn't want anywhere near the way you are memorialized? If the latter, is it still something you need to spend time on?

Empathy for Descendants

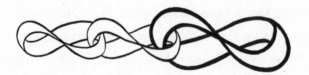

Now we're ready to link the final piece of Transgenerational Empathy, empathy for descendants. And before we go any further, let's get one thing clear: You do not have to have children to have descendants. As Mother Teresa said, "The problem with the world is that we draw the circle of our family too small." So don't take "descendants" literally. You impact the next genera-tions every day, in most things you do and decisions you make. This is not revelatory. The Iroquois Confederacy, the oldest liv-ing participatory democracy (it dates back to 1142!), declared in its founding document, "In our every deliberation, we must consider the impact of our decisions on the next seven genera-tions."[9]

Here death comes in again, because what we're really talk-ing about when we talk about being good ancestors, of course, is legacy. If death is what gives our life meaning, then legacy is what gives our death meaning.

Longpath helps us to make peace with death, because it brings us a sense of continuity through our legacies. It helps us understand that we all have an impact, that our actions and way of being—our imprint—can help advance the starting line for future generations. Imagine if each generation didn't have to start anew on the starting line of self-knowledge and actu-alization? That by individuals doing the work—by everyone doing the work—we could advance societal evolution at warp speed? Just imagine what moving the starting line so dramati-cally could mean for *Homo sapiens* in the year 5000 AD.

The care we show for future generations is the ultimate linking of the chain; it's what reconciles egoic and biological death. We may be dead in the "hardware" sense, but our "software" continues to evolve and improve with each successive generation. When we feel our impact on future generations, we are guided to be better in the present. We don't "do better" because we have guilt, but because we realize that we're playing a role in helping *them* be better. We are playing a role in what I think of as The Project: making a better *Homo sapiens* for the next ten thousand years.

Unlike all other creatures, humans alone have the capability of understanding our place in time, and in history. While all mammals have an awareness that there is a here and now, and a form of memory, and a basic awareness of the future, what makes humans' understanding of the future so different is that we can imagine multiple possibilities and plan for them years in advance. We do this when we say yes to a marriage proposal, or when we enroll in school to become a trained professional, or when we make an offer on a house we imagine our future selves (and our future babies) living in. We use our memories of the past to write plausible futures. Because of this, we alone are capable of creating the tomorrows we want to live in and, most important, the tomorrows we want our future descendants to inhabit.

There is a rich body of research about this human ability—called future consciousness. Dr. Tom Lombardo, one of the field's luminaries, posits that future consciousness was evident even in our earliest prehistoric ancestors. Whereas now we might look at a seating area in an open house and think, "I think I'll go to a garage sale and look for futons for this space," our *Australopithecus* and *Homo habilis* predecessors would think, "If I can create a round tool that I can pick up easily, it sure would make eating mash easier." They could plan, and then take behavioral steps to execute on that plan. Future consciousness gives us an evolutionary edge, because if we can plan for different versions of the future, we are more likely to survive it.

Just because we have the capacity to plan for the future doesn't mean we're any good at it, particularly when it comes to predicting how we'll feel. Research shows we're terrible at anticipating what will make even our *selves* happy in the future.[10] How are we supposed to imagine what will make our descendants happy? We need to improve at both if we are to be great ancestors.

Let's start with imagining our future selves first, because you have to run a 5K before you run a marathon. Imagine who you were a decade ago—your food preferences, your musical tastes, your foibles, and your strengths. Now imagine who you will be ten years from now. What will you like then? What kind of artists will you listen to? What kind of birthday cake will you request? If you are like most people, it's much easier to look at how you've changed and grown the *past* ten years than to imagine how you will change and grow in the *next* ten. Researchers—including Daniel Gilbert, who wrote the best-selling book *Stumbling on Happiness*—have named this phenomenon "the end of history illusion." It boils down to this: At any given point, we think that we will continue to be who we are. We're sure our preferences, values, even musical tastes won't change in the future, even though they've changed quite a bit in the past. Even as we judge who we once were, Gilbert has noted that "[w]hat we never seem to realize is that our future selves will look back and think the very same thing about us. At every age, we think we're having the last laugh, and at every age, we're wrong." [11] The same goes for humans over the past few hundred—if not thousand—years. We always think "our" generation is the greatest ever.

There's actually some very cool brain imaging that happens when you imagine your future self. The brain is pretty good at differentiating between notions of self and notions of others, but when you look to the future, your brain sees your future self as if it's watching another person. So when I imagine my birthday party twenty years from now, I see (or rather my brain sees) Future Ari as if I were looking at some uncle or a character in a play. I don't *feel* like him, and so I don't feel as well *for* him. It would be great, though, if I could, because then I'd make better decisions today to take care of him. [12] Research psychologist Hal Hershfield and his colleagues probed this issue. They invited participants to a lab and made a digital image of each person's face. They then had the participants wear 3D virtual reality goggles, so they could occupy the world of their own digital image. Participants saw themselves in the mirror, their image moving when they did, pausing when they paused; you get the idea. For half of them, their digital image was aged; when they looked in the mirror, they saw a much older version of themselves. Two weeks later, they invited participants back into the lab and asked them to invest in a hypothetical savings account. How much would they like to put away *now* for the benefit of their *future* self? Those participants who had seen an older version of themselves put twice as much money aside for the future as those who saw a present-day version of themselves. Why? Because they could better imagine what it was to *be* older.

Imagined futures and regulated emotions are critical links between who we are today and who we want to be tomorrow. They help guide and assess our future actions. Consider my love of ice cream. When I stand before my fridge and grab an apple over ice cream, scientists used to think that was all about the work of my frontal lobe, the part of my brain involved in executive functioning. But there's another part of my brain lighting up during this decision, too—the right temporoparietal junction (rTPJ). And that part of my brain is all about empathy and selflessness. In this case, Springtime Ari, looking at that ice cream pint, is able to put it back because he has empathy for Summertime Ari, who is not going to want to put on his swim shorts if he's spent the springtime immersed in his freezer. Retailers use these ideas, known in psychology circles as affective forecasting or anticipatory emotion, all the time when they market products. They want to help consumers imagine how they will *feel* with the soft skin that the foamy bath wash promises. When shoppers can tap into that future, they are more likely to cough up cash in the moment.[13]

The takeaway? Because we don't all have access to aged virtual reality versions of ourselves, we need to find ways to feel closer to our future selves and our future descendants. We need a vessel for some mental time travel—so that we can make decisions that benefit them in the future, and us today.

Concrete representations of the future are hugely helpful, it turns out. In a study out of Japan, groups were tasked with making a choice between a more sustainable or less sustainable solution, such as how to divide a pile of money or how many resources to take for the current generation. Some groups had a designated representative from a future generation, and others did not. The groups with an imaginary future generation representative chose the sustainable option 60 percent of the time. If someone from that next generation wasn't "present"? Only 28 percent of the time.[15] The Japanese are also known for what's called Future Design, wherein local residents of a town are given ceremonial robes to wear as they discuss town planning issues, imagining themselves as residents from 2060. Wales has a Future Generations Commissioner, who looks at the impact of legislation from a viewpoint of at least thirty years out, and Sweden has a Minister of the Future.

We can learn from these endeavors and improve on them.

What if the US had a Department of the Future, with a budget as large as the Defense Department's, working on issues before they became massive problems? Imagine if there was a nursery with a huge window right on the floor of Congress so lawmakers could literally see who was being impacted by decisions? What if the babies were their own children or grandchildren? Every business boardroom could have a chair set aside, too, for just this purpose. In meetings at Amazon, even small ones, an empty chair is supposed to be set aside that represents "the customer." [16] Now imagine if at every major board meeting, be it for a large corporation like Amazon or a small nonprofit like a neighborhood food bank, an empty chair was set aside to represent future generations and their needs?

At my house, we do this on a small scale. On our mantel, along with photos of my parents and Sharon's parents, and photos of us and of the kids, we have placed empty frames for the generation to come. And every Passover, while it's traditional to set an empty place for the prophet Elijah, we set a place for our descendants. Passover may well be when I feel my place as a link in the chain most strongly—seeing those empty frames, and that empty chair, awaiting their humans; hearing my kids' voices reading the Haggadah just as their ancestors did; tasting the brisket that is Sharon's family recipe . . . these nights, for me, are when Transgenerational Empathy is easiest, when I have the most *felt* sense of the practice. These are the moments when I think of how wise my dad was when he said that to get revenge on Hitler, he wanted not to kill him but to have children.

At Longpath Labs, we created a narrative anchoring exercise that is designed to inspire this same sense of empathy for the future, to bring the threads of Transgenerational Empathy together, but in a secular sense. We ask participants to first consider generations that are alive now.

Post–World War II generation: Members of Baby Boomers will be alive 1946–2060.

Accelerated culture generation: Members of Gen X will be alive 1961–2079.

New millennium generation: Members of Millennials will be alive 1980–2094.

Instant connection generation: Members of Zoomers will be alive 1995–2109.

Think about the defining influences of these four generations. Think of what's changed during their lifetimes. Think of what's important to them. How do you relate to each of them? Now, what can you imagine the *next* four generations will be like? What are they called? What do they do? What character traits and purpose define them? What do they struggle with? What do you think they'll need to collectively thrive?

Don't immediately go to a dark place as you imagine the future. If we think of climate crisis and nuclear war and Hunger

Games, our potential for connection and empathy will be compromised before it's even forged. Try, instead, feeling future generations' joy. Their awe. Their gratitude. If we really think about it, we have a good amount of knowledge about the needs of our descendants. We have a good sense of what we should be doing, and *not* doing, to earn their respect, and maybe even their thanks.

LET'S GO AHEAD and name those next four generations:

The _____ Generation: Members of Generation _____ will be alive 2010–2129

The _____ Generation: Members of Generation _____ will be alive 2030–2144

The _____ Generation: Members of Generation _____ will be alive 2045–2159

The _____ Generation: Members of Generation _____ will be alive 2060–2175

Choose a generation from your list above and picture your own version of a descendant from that era. Perhaps you'd like to give them a personal name. Now ask yourself the following questions:

What message do you have for your descendant?

What ethics and values do you hope they will carry on in their own lives?

How would your descendant view a decision you made today?

What internal work are you doing, or do you need to do, that they will thank you for?

What do you hope they'll leave behind or move beyond?

What regrets do you have to share? What words of inspiration?

I'm being very prescriptive about all of this, because empathy for the future takes some practice to get used to. But the goal, as with the entire transgenerational trio, is that it becomes your subconscious, default way of being. Past, present, and future are with you all the time. It's like you're a superhero, with three different powers wrapped up in every decision you make, large or small. Now imagine where you could go.

In the next chapter, let's go there.

CHAPTER 4 | CREATING

Futures and How
We Make Them

[W]hen, even in the imaginary future—a space where the mind can stretch beyond the Milky Way to envision routine space travel, cuddly space animals, talking apes, and time machines—people can't fathom a person of non-Euro descent a hundred years into the future, a cosmic foot has to be put down.

—YTASHA L. WOMACK

When we think about futures, we usually borrow from a construct known as the Official Future: a shared set of (usually unvoiced) assumptions about what's going to happen. We take as givens, for instance, that prices will fluctuate due to supply and demand, that children will receive formal education in their early years, that politicians will kiss babies and tell half-truths, that there will always be the haves and the have-nots. The future is intractable; it's something that just *is*.

We've always had forces writing the Official Future for us, and if we're honest with ourselves, most of us like it that way. We like clear rules and guidelines for succeeding in life: If you're good, you're going to Heaven, and if you're bad, you're going to Hell; if you go to university, you'll get a good job, and if you don't, you'll be stuck in a dead-end trap. "[L]iving with a radically open future is cognitively exhausting," wrote historian and scholar Nils Gilman; "people crave a sense of certainty about the future, which is precisely what the Official Future is meant to provide." We *want* someone, somehow, somewhere laying out the rules of the game, and what it is we need to do to play it well so we can end up on top (or at least not smushed on the bottom). The Official Future supplies a semblance of coherence; it gives us goals and eases our angst about tomorrow. Remember from the last chapter—humans are capable of thinking about tomorrow—so it follows we want to also *know, predict, and control* tomorrow, even though these abilities are often seemingly beyond our reach.

While a version of an Official Future exists in all cultures, in the West, our current narrative comes from the Enlightenment, the Scientific Revolution, and the Industrial Revolution. The way we think about the future is based solidly in the primacy of logic, the reverence for science, and a strong sense of individualism. The Official Future story we tell today is that logic, rationality, and things that we can see and measure are what count toward ensuring human progress. At the core? The belief that humans (especially genius masterminds) can anticipate and conquer nature by using intellect and technology. It is the job of titans of industry and world leaders to build (or precolonize) the world that we will one day inhabit.

This Official Future narrative is powerful in determining the direction of our lives. For instance, the cars you drive and the roads you drive on have grounding in, among other places, the 1939 World's Fair themed "World of Tomorrow," which had prominent exhibitions from car makers like General Motors and Ford. The story of the Official Future they told was that cars would get people to important places. And, most important, that cars and roads were the "next step" on the march to human progress. That story helped to inspire the Federal Aid Highway Act, wherein forty-one thousand miles of highway were constructed within ten years. The power of the Official Future is that it always contains a strong vision of the world to come. That vision can be utopian (like the propaganda posters the Soviet Union had plastered all over the Moscow subways during the Cold War), dystopian (environmental organizations' fundraising letters with polar bears swimming in the open ocean), or somewhere in between (see any magazine that contains new fad diet ads). Now technology and science has evolved beyond just cars, and so has the Official Future narrative. (If this planet putters out, no worries, we can colonize Mars! Having an existential crisis? There's an app for that!) But there's a problem with the salve of the Official Future: It doesn't work. And it especially doesn't work in an Intertidal, when the rules of the previous paradigm are failing.

There's general agreement among so-called Futurists like me that the concept of one, unifying Official Future is cracking. Most people can see this when they look closely at our current Official Future narrative about technology: It doesn't seem to make us free, happy, and able to rise above existential threats. Teens, avid consumers of tech, have experienced increased suicide rates every year since 2007.[1] Doctors have more and more high-tech tools to help manage their practices, but are also reporting high rates of burnout.[2] Sea levels are still rising, infectious diseases are increasing in frequency, and forests are burning at an epic scale. Tech even created the ecosystem that enabled the manipulation of the US political system, as a 2018 report released by the Senate explained: "Social media have gone from being the natural infrastructure for sharing collective grievances and coordinating civic engagement, to being a computational tool for social control, manipulated by canny political consultants and available to politicians in democracies and dictatorships alike."[3]

When we notice that technology does not always save the day, it becomes clear how flawed the notion of a singular Official Future itself is. Though the Official Future provides comfort because it places everything in society within a larger story—in other words, creates order within chaos—it isn't real. What happens when that Official Future starts to crack? When the "story of us" falls apart because its own logic no longer makes sense? The solution is the second pillar of Longpath: thinking more creatively and inclusively about the future.

THINK ABOUT THE CULTURE and society that you live and work within. What Official Future stories or themes do you recognize? What do you accept as "just being the way it is"? Where did these expectations come from? How might they affect what you believe is possible?

Flexing Our Futuring Capacity

There are a lot of lofty academic terms that get thrown around when we talk about the work of futuring or futures thinking: words like *foresight, prospection, prefactuals, backcasting,* and *mental simulation.* The approach feels theoretical, when really, futuring is something we already do all the time, just not necessarily in a targeted way. In a study conducted by social psychologist Roy Baumeister and his colleagues, participants reported that they thought about the future three times more than they did the past and that almost a third of their everyday thoughts related to the present day had implications for the future.[4] Trouble is, that future we're thinking about is often our near future (our short-termism): the laundry that needs to be picked up, the dentist appointment next week, or taxes that need to be filed. If we want to move beyond an Official Future that someone else decided for us and that considers more than the next two steps forward, we have to practice futuring for ourselves. It's not so hard, and there are even times that we do this naturally.

For instance, let's imagine a young woman, we'll call her Nyesa, who has just accepted a marriage proposal, and let's pretend we can see inside her heart and her mind. First, at a very deep level, she is ecstatic about joining her life with her love's, and she said yes to her partner because she was able to imagine a wonderful future together, the adventures they'd go on, and all of life's transitions that they'd see through hand-in-hand. As soon as these lovebirds announce their engagement, some Official Future expectations start bubbling up. Her mother starts rooting around in the attic for the heirloom veil that she wants Nyesa to wear, her future mother-in-law hints that grandchildren shouldn't be too far behind the wedding date, and her dear old dad calls up his parish's pastor to check on the chapel's availability, even though neither Nyesa nor her partner is religious. And that's just the beginning. Before this pair can even think twice about what would be the best expression of their love for each other and how to articulate their commitment before their friends and families, they've been hijacked. Bridal magazines, wedding planners, caterers, bakers, dressmakers, jewelers, event spaces, and Pinterest boards all convene to push a version of this wedding that will ultimately help contribute to an industry profiting $50 to 80 billion a year in the US alone.[5]

Nyesa's had enough. She and her fiancée decide to silence their phones and sit on a park bench with a notebook. They talk through their experiences at weddings in the past and laugh about wedding scenes they've watched on television or at the movies. They make a list of some of the wedding traditions that feel meaningful to them that they actually want to carry on. When setting a date, they think back and remember that for the past several years, wildfire seasons typically pop up at the end of dry summers, so they make a projection forward to set a date that is in the late spring instead. An outdoor wedding feels more authentic to them (sorry, Dad!), and they want to avoid air that is choked with smoke. Given the variability of temperatures at that time of year, Nyesa and her partner decide to serve a light dinner to their guests in case they need to get up frequently to warm up or cool off during the reception. And speaking of guests, Nyesa suddenly remembers that her Uncle Tre shouldn't be seated anywhere near his ex-husband if they want to maintain good vibes during the event.

Nyesa and her partner run through multiple mental simulations of the day, a process that is highly emotional for them both. Nyesa imagines how her fiancée will look, the way she will probably cry saying her vows, the expressions on her parents' faces, what it will be like to have everyone she loves most in the world in the same place and at the same time, and how it will feel one day, sitting with her great-grandkids on her lap, describing how this was just the beginning of her love story. Her heart swells with hope.

All of these thoughts, emotions, and desires work together to drive the decisions and compromises that Nyesa and her partner make about their wedding, and the steps that they will take to enact the future that they want. They push through the burden of Official Future expectations, and co-create a version that is both reflective and supportive of their love. Throughout this process, though Nyesa has barely broken a sweat, she has been exercising both futures thinking and the Transgenerational Empathy that we talked about in the last chapter. We all have this capacity. It's just there. It's like muscles on the bone. We just need to flex these skills from time to time, and sometimes we need some extra endurance training so that we're applying all of our futuring skills for the good of those great-grandkids sitting on Nyesa's lap. This is how we take the *Homo sapiens* ability of prospection, or futures thinking, and direct it not only toward an individual wedding, or even an individual life, but toward human flourishing writ large.

How to Co-Create the Future: The Second Pillar of Longpath

Futures thinking requires intentionality. If we are going to be around in ten thousand years, we need to get ourselves together and decide a) that we actually *want* to be here then, and b) what we want the world to look and feel like. And I do not just mean the technology; I mean the insides of our hearts and minds. If we don't get that together now, I doubt we will be here in one thousand years—let alone ten thousand years.

We are so primed to think about what we *don't* want. Our representations of the future tend to be dystopian, of the *Handmaid's Tale, 1984, Brave New World,* and *Terminator* variety. We take these warnings and focus on how to run away from their eventuality. But we don't talk nearly enough about what we want to move toward. The former feels familiar to us. We all suffer from what's known as negativity bias—we let the bad things captivate our attention and tend to downplay the good things. Often we make decisions based on those negative perceptions. The latter—thinking about what's possible—feels daring, like we're venturing off the Official Future railway and into a wild, wild west.

This process of bringing intentionality and agency to the future can be intimidating, but it's also very freeing. Once you realize the "Official Future" is in quotes, you realize that anything is possible, that there are actually multiple places we could end up on the other side of the Intertidal. What's more, nobody is creating the future alone. We're all contributing, whether it be through our action or our nonaction. We're all living in and responding to past and present events as the to-morrows emerge. The beautiful thing about the topsy-turvy nature of an Intertidal is that what we do now can have expo-nential effects on what comes later. I'll spare you the chaos and complexity theory behind this statement and summarize by saying that even small actions can lead to great effects (SAGE, my favorite acronym!) and that our futures are open, dynamic, and emergent, not prefabricated.

The question is this: How do we influence the future in a democratic, participatory way, so that no one entity, industry, or even religion is in charge of dictating to us what "the fu-ture" will be? How do we support the future so it is multifac-eted, always improving, and we *all* cowrite it? The Longpath answer is to do away with the word *future* in the singular, in favor of *futures*. There's not one predetermined way forward, there are many, and each is in constant mix and match and in-ventive play with the next. There's no Official Future; there are emergent, Participatory Futures. If an Official Future is a formal and scripted orchestral arrangement, then Participatory Futures are the best jazz set you have ever heard. The interplay between the parts of the system and the process itself becomes part of what makes it magical.

I'm hardly the first futurist to suggest that we don't need

to follow an Official Future. It's kind of our vocation's calling card, actually. A futurist named Joseph Voros put a great image to it with the Voros cone—also known as the futures cone, which I've adapted somewhat for Longpath Labs.

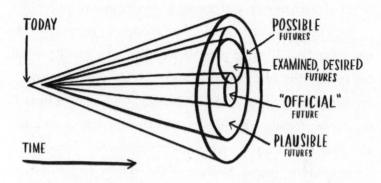

The Voros cone shows how there is more or less a straight line between what we do today and an "official future." We can look at the Voros cone with a civilizational lens, but let's start with the individual. One individual in particular, whom we'll call Tim.

Tim grew up in an insular community in conservative Russell, Kansas. The *official future* that he, his family, and community subscribe to is that he will marry a nice girl, get a stable job, have a couple of kids, vote conservative, go to church regularly, take care of his parents, and eventually die from heart disease like most males in his family.

Now, what happens if we expand from the constricted,

Longpath

official future into a more open cone and look at one of the *plausible futures* for Tim? Tim is restless, and while he doesn't know just what he wants, he does know he wants to leave Russell. But how? He sets his sights on becoming a NASCAR driver, a really popular sport in his world. Being a driver will enable him to travel, earn money, and choose a broader palette for his life.

Let's open the cone even further, though, to get to a *possible future* for Tim. What is possible for Tim, if he really pushed the limits? Tim loves to cook, and is pretty good at it, so it's feasible that instead of NASCAR being his ticket out of Russell (he doesn't actually like the sport), it's cooking school. Or medical school. Or maybe even music. His possible futures have some limits, of course, because of the tectonic forces or drivers of change of the world he's living in—at the societal level, we futurists call these megatrends. Tim would be hard-pressed to start a newspaper, for instance, because the megatrend that everything is being digitized means that another print press probably isn't sustainable. (For more on Longpath megatrends, see page 171.)

Now, even as Tim pushes the envelope to imagine what's possible, he's not done yet. While Tim might have a possible future as a cook, he hasn't really examined that future. He likes cooking better than driving, but is that what he really wants to do? What is aligned with his deepest-seated values? What would make his days—at work and outside of it—feel meaningful? Yes, it sounds cheesy, but what would make his heart

110

sing? And what would he want future generations to think about how he spent his life? Creating examined, desired futures requires looking not just forward but back, and analyzing the forces that brought him to his conclusions in the first place. It requires blending the Voros cone with the Mobius chain from following chapters. The New School professor and design researcher Elliott Montgomery got to this concept with his reimagining of the Voros cone as one that includes the past.

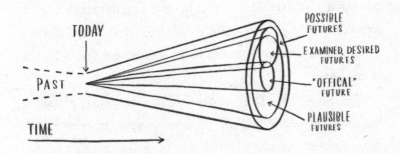

When Tim really examines what got him to where he is, a young man in Russell, Kansas, the fourth-generation Timothy in his family, he is able to see how many assumptions he actually has about how to be in the world. He sees how he has unquestioningly bought into an Official Future, and how his ancestors did, too. He is able to see why he thinks about the future in the way that he does—the way the media, his church, his teachers, and his parentage make him think he needs to be Christian, heterosexual, and the main financial provider for an eventual family. From there, he can separate out what he actually wants. And he is able to see that what he *really* wants is to spend his days outside, immersed in nature. He has always been happiest when his family vacationed in the Rocky Mountains. He imagines skiing down a hill, the wind in his face. He has always felt a great sense of purpose when helping others, and so he wonders about teaching skiing, perhaps even to those who are physically limited in some way, like combat amputees or kids with physical challenges. What if he could help someone learn to ski who never thought they'd get to experience the freedom of flying down a hill? What if he could help, in some small way, to open their minds to what's possible, just as his has been opened?

We are all like Tim, to one extent or another, grappling with official, plausible, and possible futures. In John Lane's book *Timeless Simplicity,* he tells the following parable:

> *The industrialist was horrified to find the fisherman lying beside his boat, smoking a pipe.*
>
> *"Why aren't you fishing?" asked the industrialist.*
>
> *"Because I've caught enough fish for the day."*
>
> *"Why don't you catch some more?"*
>
> *"What would I do with them?"*
>
> *"Earn more money. Then you could have a motor fixed to your boat and go into deeper waters and catch more fish.*

That would bring you money to buy nylon nets, so more fish,
more money. Soon you would have enough to buy two boats,
even a fleet of boats, then you could be rich like me."

"What would I do then?"

"Then you could sit back and enjoy life."

"What do you think I'm doing now?"[6]

Like the Tims of the world, the industrialist was following the path to an *official future*, without examining why he was headed there in the first place. There's scientific grounding for what was going on with the industrialist: hedonic adaptation, also known as the hedonic treadmill. Hedonic adaptation suggests that people repeatedly return to a baseline level of happiness, no matter what they buy or achieve. What this means is that the industrialist keeps acquiring more in order to get a happiness boost. And when it fades? He wants more again. And so he works harder and harder to get happiness, staying put on the treadmill of his life, without really examining what got him there and where it's leading him. If he could see outside himself, he might just notice how he's not really going anywhere, and he might even decide to stop working altogether and apply his energy elsewhere.

We're beginning to examine the treadmill collectively, too. In an environment where 60 percent of college students said they were too anxious to enjoy life,[7] Yale professor Laurie

Kids Book

Santos created a course about happiness. It's by far the most popular course the school has had in its three-hundred-year history. If the *official future* of the kids at Yale—who, according to the equation of what equals a good life, are *winning*—it's a harbinger that we all might be ready for a new equation altogether. After all, who wants a future with such high levels of stress and anxiety? Who wants a life that is unbearable?

TAKE A FEW MOMENTS to work through the Voros cone for yourself. What do you see as your Official Future? What causes and conditions led to that probable outcome? Now take a breath. A deep one. Shake out your shoulders a little bit. Relax your jaw. Take the tongue off the roof of your mouth. Let your mind branch out a little bit to consider some plausible futures. These may be a bit of a stretch for you, but usually you can see yourself in a plausible future. Is there an image or memory coming to mind? Can you use your senses to describe what is coming up for you? Maybe take a few moments to jot down some notes. At this point, you may notice that your mind is trying to redirect your attention or you may hear some doubt or negative self-talk. See if you can set the naysayers aside and let yourself drift a bit further. Some of you may find that this is as far as you can go, and that's fine, but if you're willing to play a little bit more, let's open the scope of your imagination to invite in some ideas or feelings that may feel like a total fantasy but are still possible futures for you. Let them be totally outrageous if that's fun for you. Try softening your eyes and letting the corners of your mouth turn upward slightly, as if to smile. See if you can tap into some possible futures that make you feel warm-hearted, accepted, excited, or curious. What are some of the ingredients that are showing up in these possible futures? How wide is your Voros cone stretching? How does it feel to push the boundaries of what's possible?

The Examined, Desired Future

Socrates proclaimed, "The unexamined life is not worth living." To this, I'd humbly add that the unexamined future is not worth fighting for.

Perhaps my greatest objective as a futurist—beyond pushing people to think further than their own life span—is to get them to pressure-test their desired futures, to look at where they're really coming from. Are they thinking of Participatory Futures, not just one Official Future? Are they considering a desired future that they have fully examined, or one they have unwittingly internalized along the way? We can apply these questions on the individual level, on the industry level, on the societal level, and on the civilizational level.

On the individual level, consider the issue of attention deficit hyperactivity disorder (ADHD). The diagnosis rate dramatically increased in just twenty years—from 6.1 percent to 10.2 percent.[8] And medication for it has been prescribed in commensurate numbers. Now, the *official future* for a kid named Kiron with untreated ADHD is that he will struggle some. His grades may suffer, as might his self-esteem. The *desired future* for Kiron is that he will be super successful, at school and therefore at life, and so he starts taking Adderall to make that desired future more likely.

This, however, is not an *examined desired future*. For that, we need to go a layer deeper, further back in time, and further forward in time. Kiron might well have ADHD, but his father had it, too, and so did his grandmother. ADHD wasn't diagnosed back in the day, and it wasn't really an issue for them— his grandmother didn't attend school past eighth grade, and his dad had plenty of outlets for his energy and he charmed his teachers into giving him grades that were good enough. ADHD might not be an issue for Kiron, either, except what is expected of him now is quite different from what was expected of his grandmother sixty years ago or his dad thirty years ago—he needs to sit at a desk for six hours a day and then do two hours of homework at night, especially if he is going to get the grades he thinks he needs to be competitive and get into college, so he can get a job sitting behind a desk eight hours a day. . . . It's also much easier for Kiron to be diagnosed than it would have been for his grandma or dad. Professionals are aware of and can pinpoint neurological differences and prescribe medication to work around them.

Now we need to go forward in time. What will Kiron's kids and grandkids face? Likely, they will have even more tools at their disposal—genetic enhancements, speed testing for learning or behavioral "abnormalities"—to get them closer to some version of peak performance. So is peak performance the end goal? Who decides what peak performance actually is? Is the examined desired future one where everyone is entirely neurotypical? Or is the examined desired future one with a neurodiverse human population, where your brain doesn't have to be wired in one particular way in order to have a happy and productive life? What does success look like in each of these futures? Are we conforming to an Official Future written by someone with a vested interest in keeping us locked into that narrative for a reason that benefits them . . . or us?

Again, we might argue about *what* the best future is—but we need to ask the question. Kiron may decide to take medication because of the expectations of his environment, but take pains to move out of that environment in time, and then to change it. The next year might find him in a different place, with different questions altogether. In the Talmudic tradition, we say that people should *always* question—that the questions should never stop. This way, the solutions always get better. An examined desired future is a process, not a definitive endpoint.

Let's apply this concept not to an individual's functioning in the world, but to an industry's.

Imagine being a fly on the wall of a car company, where the *official future* is one where they keep growing their business and increasing their profit. Executives are naturally focused on new cars that can meet people's needs. The company is open to electrification and is excited to be part of a new frontier of decreased carbon emissions. The problem they're tackling: How can we make sure electric cars can go four hundred miles on a single charge, because that's what consumers want?

This electric vehicle vision is a *desired future,* one where we have fewer carbon emissions. But it's not an *examined* desired future. Do we want more efficient cars, or do we actually want more efficient ways of getting around? Before investing countless hours and dollars in infrastructure that supports electric vehicles, is this company considering why it assumes individuals need cars in the first place? An *examined desired future,* then, might be one that factors in the movement afoot in Europe to create "fifteen-minute cities"—communities where you can get anywhere you regularly need to go, such as school, hospital, grocery stores, or work, within fifteen minutes by bike or on foot. That doesn't mean this car company will be obsolete. Communities will still have mobility needs, and this company can play an important role in meeting those needs. But first, they need to get out of their box of thinking about one set future that is driven by their corporate interests in order to fully see themselves as part of an examined desired future that is inclusive of their broader communities.

The same thinking applies—but is even more complex—when it comes to entities that are tasked with solving some of our world's biggest problems, like hunger, poverty, or the plight of refugees. While the car company can always have a purpose, the *examined desired future* of a nonprofit charged with ending hunger should logically be for that NGO not to need to exist at all. But so many nonprofits that I've consulted with over the years can't get there. They're busy managing immediate crises, which is understandable, but also frustrating. When I have suggested that, in addition to stanching the bleeding, they build processes so that they no longer have to exist, they struggle to see alternate futures. Their *official future* is very dystopian: There will always be hunger/poverty/refugees, and in fact it's going to get worse. That's the way it is. My argument is that yes, it might take decades, but we have to start with an *examined desired future*; otherwise we surely will never get there.

It's like the "working backwards" method championed by the likes of Steve Jobs, wherein a company starts a new product development process with a faux press release from a day—way out into the future—when the product greets the world. They start with the vision, centered on their goal of delighting the customer, and then work backwards to make it happen. How can these NGO entities be doing their jobs if they're not at least aiming for a world where their services don't need to exist? What is the faux press release from the day they are no longer needed? What does that desired future look like?

LET'S GO BACK FOR a moment and look at our Voros cone from the last exercise. What was your Official Future? What was your examined, desired future? Can you put it into a collectively examined context? In other words, if you were to place your desired future in the center of an interconnected web of other desired futures, what would need to be true in the world for those to manifest? What would that world look and feel like? What is your World's Fair World of Tomorrow like for society?

Okay, now let's take the notion of futures further out from the individual and industrial to the civilizational. Imagine what would happen if we could meet together as *Homo sapiens*, all eight billion of us. Our *official future* might look like what all the NGOs see: a dystopian mess where it's every human for themselves. A *desired future* might be one where power is distributed, where there is social justice, and where gaps between rich and poor are negligible.

An *examined desired future* is one where power itself looks very different. It's one where perhaps we imagine an environment that allows every individual to maximize their talents to make the world better for the next generation and still be happy and well-resourced. Material success may well be a part of this examined desired future, not in the service of the manufacturers and marketers, but ensuring that everyone can flourish. People have a broad sense of agency and can express the best possible version of themselves. Technology may well also be a part of this examined desired future, not in strict service to its shareholders but, again, to everyone. Maybe it's a world where we make spiritual and psychological progress every day. Maybe it's a world where we continue questioning futures, and we strive not just for faster computers, but for bigger hearts and more discerning minds.

The point is, we have an *ultimate aim* or, to use the original Greek term, a *telos*. Telos asks one of the most fundamental questions of existence: "To what end?"

Our Ithaca

In *The Odyssey*, Odysseus spends ten years at war and then ten years finding his way home. His telos was pretty clear: He was imagining Ithaca and his love, Penelope. No matter which way the wind blew him, he always knew where he was heading. In *Man's Search for Meaning*, psychiatrist and Holocaust survivor Viktor Frankl writes of how in Nazi concentration camps, "those who knew that there was a task waiting for them to fulfill were most apt to survive." He had a personal telos: a publication-ready manuscript he'd written had been confiscated, and he wanted to rewrite it. When he had typhus during his imprisonment, he wrote notes to help him in the work of his rewriting. "I am sure that this reconstruction of my lost manuscript in the dark barracks of a Bavarian concentration camp assisted me in overcoming the danger of cardiovascular collapse," he wrote.[9]

Now imagine telos at a civilizational level. What are we working toward? The Second Coming of Christ? The Messiah? The singularity where humans and machines merge into one? Something else? And when and where can we even have that conversation at a global level?

Telos is integral to Longpath's second pillar, as it is the purpose—even if it evolves—of all of our efforts. It's the "why" we do what we do. We know we want futures that are desired and that we need to constantly examine those desired futures. But what do we check those examined futures against? Like Odysseus, we need an Ithaca. Some say we've lost it, while I'm not sure we had an Ithaca to begin with. We need one, though, so that regardless of what the world throws at us, we stay on target. This is telos. It's the goal above all of the trends and megatrends of life.

I'm going to be bold here and assume a common telos for all the readers of this book: I'm going to assume you want a better us—a *Homo sapiens* species that is better than our cousin from a half million plus years ago and better than who we are now, a species that has the compassion of Mother Teresa, the intelligence of Einstein, and the collaborative spirit of the two million people a year who volunteer for Habitat for Humanity. You probably want a world where we are still wholly human (as opposed to a bunch of AI-assisted cyborgs), only better, so we can eradicate unnecessary suffering and intergenerational trauma. You probably want a world where we can maximize human potential at the individual and societal level and maintain a healthy and vibrant home planet Earth for generations to come.

Right about now is where people typically get tripped up. *That's all well and good, Ari, but how the hell are we supposed to get there?* Well, first of all, telos is not a place so much as it's a horizon. So you don't actually ever get there in some magical, utopic sense. And second, to borrow a phrase from Peter Block, the answer to "how?" is "yes." You just do it, with care and attention. Telos is the mechanism, the magnetic true north, that allows you to align your actions and decision points toward your ultimate end. You need only ask, "Is this aligned with my telos?" to help shift your trajectory. When we use telos in the boardroom, it gives birth to food and beverage companies like Rebbl, which seeks to end human trafficking and uplift the lives of survivors; travel companies like Playa Viva, which created an organic agricultural system that benefited not just the resort but also the surrounding area; and clothing companies like Jackalo, which buys back the clothes it sells after kids have outgrown them and then renews, resells, or recycles them.

THINK OF A CRISIS, or even just a knotty problem, that you're facing. It could be through your work or something you're dealing with on the home front. As you seek solutions, what would it look like to have two lenses? Can you find an immediate solution that mitigates the problem, and another solution that plants a carob seed for the future? Can these be the same solution? What if you used these lenses for all of your major problem-solving?

When I used telos after I got the notification about Ruby's Spanish assignment, back in Chapter 1, I was able to push away my short-termist, peer-pressure-fueled worry about Ruby's future. I knew not only what I didn't want—a fight with my daughter that would inevitably push us to separate corners—but what I *did* want. I wanted a world where grades were relegated to their rightful place as secondary, a world where our kids, too, understood that their grades didn't define them, but that how they showed up for others did. When Michelle of the sports track used telos, she thought not just of how she wanted a sports facility built to last, but how she wanted a world where "built to last" was the default way of thinking, not an aspiration, and where work product was evaluated at least in part on its social and environment impact as a matter of course. If someone were in her place hundreds of years in the future, she would have wanted that person to automatically think about *their* descendants rather than just short-term cost.

What these examples all have in common is a teleological vision of collective flourishing. Flourishing is not a static state, utopic vision, or prized ideal. It's not Gollum stroking his precious ring in a Tolkien novel. Rather, collective flourishing is a goal of sustained well-being that serves all peoples and ecologies with equity, goodness, growth, generativity, connection, meaning, resiliency, and vitality.[10] Lest this sound, well, abstract, it isn't. We can *see* it in the example of a small village near Amsterdam called Hogewey.

125

Hogewey looks like what you would expect a village to look like. It has houses, a grocery store, a park, a restaurant, a pub. It has streets and alleys and public benches. And in actuality, it's a nursing home for people with Alzheimer's disease and dementia. The cofounder of Hogewey, Yvonne van Amerongen, said she and her colleagues began the project when they realized that nursing homes for those with Alzheimer's were nothing like "real life." Instead, they were like hospitals, with dozens of people living on a closed ward. Residents were deprived of anything resembling life as they knew it, adding confusion to their already confused mental processing. So Yvonne and her cofounders pushed through the Official Future, to what was possible, desirable, and examined, and Hogewey was born.

"Everyone wants fun in life, a meaningful life," Yvonne has said. "We want to go out of our house and do some shopping and meet other people. That social life is important. It means that you're a part of society, that you belong. And that's what people need, even if you are living with advanced dementia." What Yvonne and her colleagues hit upon was an incarnation of collective flourishing, a place where dignity and humanity were centered, where residents could interact with one another and with the staff and volunteers around them in "normal" environments, and it cost no more than a traditional nursing home. "It has to do with thinking different," Yvonne said, "looking at the person in front of you and looking at what does this person need, now? And it's about a smile, it's about thinking different, it's about how you act, and that costs nothing." [12]

LET'S START THIS COLLECTIVE flourishing exercise with a long, soft gaze. Imagine the kind of fixed daydreaming that you experience when you're sitting somewhere with nothing else to do, no pressure, watching a sunrise or sunset. Maybe, out of the corner of your eye, you notice the slight curvature that happens on the distant horizon, reminding you that you are here—on Earth—spinning and traveling through space. Your problems and worries seem small in the grand scheme of things. What a miracle it is that you are here at all, as part of this natural world, looking upon the same far horizon that millions before you looked upon, and millions after you will, too. It's rather peaceful, not to have to be in control of this moment. The day will begin or end without your interference. You notice birds and insects fluttering about. Wind blowing through grass or sand. Or maybe laundry that's been hung out to dry. You ask yourself: What brings me peace? What brings me joy? What makes me feel like I belong? What makes me feel safe? What makes me feel loved?

Perhaps there are voices or other sounds piping up around you. Animals barking or traffic in the background. See if you can bring one person or creature into focus. Quietly ask them the same questions that you have been asking yourself: What brings you peace? What brings you joy? What makes you feel like you belong? What makes you feel safe? What makes you feel loved? If it feels appropriate, maybe get up and ask another person these questions out loud.

Whether the answers are real or imagined, are there any overlaps between your responses and theirs? Differences? Conflicts? Can you imagine a world where your replies can coexist? Are there any reconciliations or creative compromises that would be needed? If you have time, you may also want to try applying some Transgenerational Empathy here, and ask the same questions to a theoretical person in the far future.

So far, Longpath has involved a lot of thinking, a lot of accessing emotions, and changing mindsets. But we also need action to propel us toward the vision of the futures we want. We can't *just* think and feel our way to the Promised Land. We have to get on the path and start walking there. It's a journey that feels infinite. And so for inspiration and wisdom as to how to do this and where to begin, I turn to the story of a brilliant engineer and a small piece of metal.

Call Me Trim Tab

In World War II, the U.S. Navy commissioned inventor and futurist (and at one point, my mother's professor) Buckminster Fuller to solve a problem. As ships got bigger and bigger, they became more difficult to turn. The war effort required big ships, but also maneuverability. So Fuller invented the trim tab—a six-inch-wide strip of metal attached by hinges to the trailing edge of the ship's rudder. By leaning into the resis-

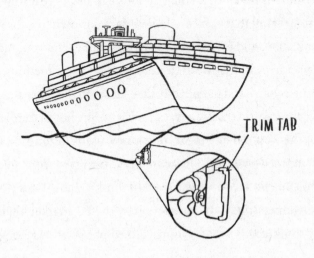

TRIM TAB

tance of oncoming water, this tiny strip of metal provided the "power" needed to swing the ship's massive rudder and thus turn an enormous ship. Fuller later used the term *trim tab* as a metaphor for human potential. If we're willing to go against the flow, a very small change can turn something very big around. His headstone, in fact, reads, "Call me Trim Tab."

The current human experience, in a way, is a battleship. It can seem like certain things are just too big to turn around at this point—we're going full steam ahead into the Official (catastrophic) Future. But if we see we should be changing direction, and if we can find strength to lean into the resistance, we *can* turn the ship—even as one person. Now imagine trim tabs at scale—everyone doing their moment-by-moment trim tabs—and how that can impact the present day and futures in particular. Suddenly, hope abounds.

Trim tabs mean that small actions can have great impacts, and something that you can do now for your own life, for your organization, and for society can ripple out beyond you. A trim tab, with an examined desired future in mind, is something that can move you—and us collectively—closer to the telos-aligned, flourishing world that you want to live in. Try not to think only about the way you buy meat substitutes, used clothing, or shop at the farmer's market. These are great trim tabs, don't get me wrong. But we are so accustomed to thinking about our power as consumers and our interaction with the market that we don't think about what Yvonne talked about with Hogewey:

the power of our interactions with other human beings. These interactions can be tender, being the type of person who offers an elderly person an arm when crossing the road, and fierce, being the type of person who stands firmly against abuses of power. Trim tabs are not ways to bypass the work of truth, reconciliation, and transformation; they are ways to start doing the work of creating a better future self, community, organization, or society immediately so that broader systemic changes emerge alongside. It's tweaking small pieces of our source code so that our default behavior algorithms work better across the board.

I'll give you a quick trim tab example. I'm a consummate multitasker. Still, I know multitasking—especially when it involves technology—affects my connection with other humans. When I think far out into the future, I want to make sure we're still feeling, we're still speaking, we're still sharing, and we're still doing all the things that make us human. One of my trim tabs is to look as many people in the eyes as I can, smile, and share a meaningful moment, even if it's just for a second while I'm letting them scan my ID at building security. I know this has a ripple effect in ways that I might not directly or immediately see. It's a way of acting now to ensure we're preserving humanity in the future. It's creating the world in which I want to live, and one that I want future generations to live in, too.

You probably already have multiple trim tabs, even if you don't call them by that name. Some of these happen at the consumption level, like what stores you buy from and what it is that you buy. Some might be things like giving your kid a hug every single morning. Some might be entirely internal, like talking back to the voice in your head that has nothing positive to share. But when we work on our trim tabs, when we go against the dominant flow, we are one step closer to turning the ship toward the future we want.

THINK BACK TO YOUR responses to the personal and collective flourishing questions that we asked in the previous exercise. What are two or three small and manageable trim tabs that you can commit to today that would support an internal change in yourself to help bring about flourishing futures? What are two or three trim tabs that would support external changes in your relationships, work, culture, or environment? Do these trim tabs have the look and feel of the type of flourishing that you're hoping to bring about? If your trim tab involves a behavior change, how do you plan to hold yourself (or your family, team, organization) accountable until your new habit has become routine?

I have a lot of optimism about the future. One of my family's favorite things to do is to watch SpaceX launches because they fill us with a sense of awe about all that humans are capable of. (Or possibly my family is just indulging me.) We *Homo sapiens* are capable of some incredible feats. If you think about it within the broad arc of history, really not that much time has passed between the Copernican era, when we first recognized that the Earth revolves around the sun, and me sitting on my couch watching a rocket launch. We are an impressive species, so we need to harness our amazingness and direct it in the right ways. We can use the moment of this Intertidal to push against our short-term impulses, to synthesize our deep past and our prospective future, and to imagine and move toward a future of collective flourishing. But no way will we get there using rugged individualism or personal ingenuity. We need to work together. And to do that, we need to find the others.

CHAPTER 5 | FLOURISHING

Working Together
for a Better World

When we know and revere the wholeness of life, we can stay alert and steady. We know there is no individual salvation. We join hands to find the ways the world self-heals.

—JOANNA MACY

I magine a steep ravine dividing two sections of inhabitable land. An individual comes along who wants to cross the ravine. They weigh their options and ultimately use a simple slackline to gingerly, carefully step their way across. In time, a few others join this individual in wanting to cross the ravine, and together they build a rope bridge. It's sturdy enough, but often needs repairs or replacement. Then the village next to the ravine meets and decides to raise funds to build a suspension bridge, one that will last generations, and that each successive generation will care for and maintain. The suspension bridge allows there to be more trade, better health practices, more connection between people. While a single human may be the catalyst for demonstrating a need and expressing a vision, for the many to benefit from the solution, we need to coordinate. In other words, if everyone in the world adopted a Longpath mindset on their own, we'd make real progress toward a desired future, but to reach peak momentum toward a world that looks and feels how we want it to, we need to work together.

The wisdom that "if you want to go fast, go alone; if you want to go far, go together" might seem obvious, but we work, think, and act counter to that view all the time. We live in a culture, particularly in America—where, ironically, our motto is, "Out of many, one"—that prizes the individual and singular effort over group cooperation. Look no further than the shelves at a bookstore, at the masses of "self-help" books about getting out of your own way, of loving your*self*, of pushing your*self*, of knowing your*self*. I'm guilty of it, too, with this book—up until this point, a large part of the Longpath message has been about working on your own internal thought processes and external actions. But we need a broader vision than the narrative rugged individualism allows. Individual purpose has to be nested within a broader overall trajectory for humanity, or what I introduced as The Project in Chapter 3.

Instead of thinking of our efforts like individual Lincoln Logs, rigidly stacked on top of one another to build a house, we need to think of our efforts more like a geodesic dome, which distributes stress evenly across the triangular lattices that make up the structure. This is a shared tension. What happens to a part affects the response of the whole, and it is in this relational tension that the geodesic form gets its impressive strength. If you're going to camp on Mount Everest, with its rapidly changing and rather hostile environments, you'll probably use a tent designed with geodesic principles. If you're trying to navigate an Intertidal and impact the whole of humanity, it might also be a good idea to learn how to situate yourself in a way that allows you to both provide and receive support during uncertain times.

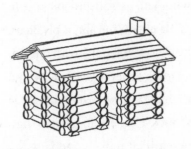 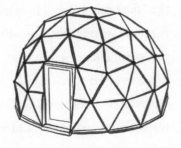

That's just what we need now as a species: to learn how to lean into our relational tension, and our interdependence, in service of making us not only stronger but also more resilient, adaptive, and creative. This is easiest when power is shared, when there is an actual distributive give-and-take. People, ideas, and cultures bumping up against each other—within a recognized whole—allow third spaces and paths to open up, for something even more exciting to emerge. Without relational tension, the world might never have met the cronut—the delicious fusion of croissant and donut. Or we might not have had the phenomenon of Lin-Manuel Miranda's musical *Hamilton*. On paper, the idea of a Broadway musical about the first secretary of the Treasury made zero sense, let alone a *hip-hop* musical. And yet, hip-hop, history, and conventional musical theater *in relationship* created a new way; a show that seemed impossible became a sensation and inspired new generations of artists and new industry models.

In Chapter 2, we talked about neuroplasticity, the discovery that the brain is capable of growing and establishing new connections throughout one's life. This chapter is about plasticity at a societal level, about changing our interactions with one another in order to make full use of our cooperative capacity and our relational tensions. Rather than a complete overhaul of our way of being, what I'm talking about are little adjustments that, at the end of the day . . . or, rather, millennium . . . add up to a different default.

We have the ability to rise, together, as a civilization, and to envision multiple futures that are co-created, emergent, and aligned with The Project of flourishing for thousands of years to come. This is not our first Intertidal, but it *is* the first Intertidal where globalization and technology have so wholly changed the game. As our world is now so hyper-connected, this is the first Intertidal where we have the knowledge, context, and wherewithal to imagine futures in a nonexploitive way . . . *or* to sow the seeds of our species' destruction through AI, nuclear war, climate, or, you know, any other garden-variety existential threat. That's why this moment of Intertidal is both terrifying and exhilarating. Because if we are to rise and improve, and not fall or regress, it is going to require a multitude of people—not just one side or one faction. To reach a critical mass, we need the Chain of Being to become interlocking Chains of Being, so that humanity—past, present, and future—resembles a lattice with any number of entry points that invite people to Longpath.

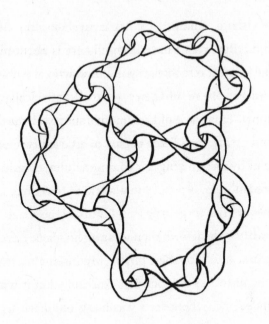

So, How Do We Do It?
How Do We Find the Others and Evolve?

Intolerance in the 23rd Century? Improbable! If man
survives that long, he will have learned to take a
delight in the essential differences between men and
between cultures. He will learn that differences in
ideas and attitudes are a delight, part of life's exciting
variety, not something to fear. It's a manifestation of
the greatness that God, or whatever it is, gave us.

—GENE RODDENBERRY, *THE MAKING OF STAR TREK*

"Find the Others" sounds a bit like a psychological thriller on first hearing. But what I have in mind here is not some secret handshake or sniff test so that you know who else thinks like you do. Rather, we're *all* Others—we all have a place in the human story. This piece of Longpath is simply about the need to remember that each "me" is part of a collective "we." The work begins by recognizing our commonalities, even in a world as fractured as ours. *Especially* in a world as fractured as ours.

Whenever I risk forgetting this, I think of the kittel. The kittel is the white robe Jewish men wear on holidays, during their wedding, and often for their burial. My mom always pointed out that the kittel has no pockets. "You don't take it with you," she reminded me, whenever I was hung up over this or that grievance or stuck on this or that perceived affront to my identity. "You leave it all on the field of life." It's a *simplifying*. The kittel reminds me that we are born into this world bare, and we leave it bare. All of us.

My good friend and Longpath Labs colleague Kimberly Streeter is a birth and death doula in her spare time, and she often talks about these moments as the most wholly human of our lives. When a safe space is created and care is offered with an informed and attuned attention, people can coexist with one another at profound levels. Current events fall away. Schedules fall away. Attachments fall away. Time itself falls away—it is like time out of time. It's going offline to reconnect with the big picture, with what's really important, and reconciling our visions of best possible outcomes. "Humans have long held rites of passage to mark significant changes in their lives," Kimberly says, "including initiations into adulthood, marriages, or transitions into parenthood. You are one thing, then you cross a threshold into a liminal in-between, and then you emerge as something else . . . something more than you were."

Traditionally, these rites of passage were accompanied by deep rituals and symbolic performances that would connect us to a vision or meaning that is larger than ourselves, and I'm not talking about the versions that are all flash and no substance. You don't need elaborate quinceañera parties with live animals, seven-tiered wedding cakes, or firework-laden gender reveals—all of which distract from the transformative meaning of the ritual. A community need only come together to acknowledge and support a passage that affects both the individual and the whole. In many ways, as Kimberly puts it, "Intertidals are humanity's rites of passage. They're our one-in-a-million chance to level-up. But this Intertidal is also the first time that we have the opportunity to recognize that we are crossing an Intertidal threshold as it's happening, giving us the chance to co-create the rules and rituals that will guide our passage and to set intentions for how we will emerge on the other side." We're all newbies here, and it's probably best if we venture out into this great unknown together.

To find the others, we can reach into these types of intersectional spaces, that recognize and build on our shared *human-*

ness, and be well on our way to living Longpath. A couple of weeks ago, I was at the park with my dog, Ozzie, when I heard an ambulance and watched it pull up a hundred feet from where I stood. Within just a few minutes, I saw EMTs doing CPR on someone on a stretcher, while what looked like a daughter and her mom stood nearby holding each other and crying. I don't know what happened after the ambulance pulled away, but having lost both my parents after unsuccessful CPR attempts, I had a strong sense that the person passed away. The incident threw me for the rest of the day. I kept thinking of the daughter and mother: *Their world has completely changed. And here I am, headed to the store to get more eggs and milk for breakfast in the morning.* I did not know them, but I felt connected to them, a strong sense of them as fellow humans dealing with all the highs and lows of life.

The next evening, I was out and about in town and came across a young mother holding her baby. This baby was brand new—maybe two weeks old. I made eye contact with the mom and pressed my hands to my heart in the universal sign for *Oh my god, isn't it amazing?* She smiled at me and nodded her head. No words were spoken between us, but we shared a moment of connection, a sense that we were fellow travelers on what Buckminster Fuller called Spaceship Earth. We affirmed through that tiny interaction that we'd both like to live in a world where complete strangers can still marvel together at the unbelievable phenomenon that is a brand-new life.

We know, thanks to the research of folks like my friend David DeSteno, that we can intentionally build on these sorts of commonalities, we can find these moments that remind us of all we share. And when we do, we are better to each other. Put another way, morality is *flexible*. David's lab did an experiment where when participants were asked to tap out the same pattern as someone else in the room, they were more apt to want to help that person with an onerous task. That's all it took: A few minutes of tapping out the same rhythm and people saw each other not as complete strangers but as fellow travelers that they wanted to give a hand up.

A famous example of humans connecting this way comes from World War I, when the German and British forces inhabited opposing trenches on the western front of the war. On Christmas Day of 1914, the two sides serenaded one another with Christmas carols, shook hands, and some met in the no-man's-land between them to play a game of soccer. As one British soldier wrote in a letter home, he heard:

> *"Come out, English soldier; come out here to us." For some*
> *little time we were cautious, and did not even answer.*
> *Officers, fearing treachery, ordered the men to be silent. But*
> *up and down our line one heard the men answering that*
> *Christmas greeting from the enemy. How could we resist*
> *wishing each other a Merry Christmas, even though we*
> *might be at each other's throats immediately afterwards? So*

*we kept up a running conversation with the Germans, all the
while our hands ready on our rifles. Blood and peace, enmity
and fraternity—war's most amazing paradox. The night
wore on to dawn—a night made easier by songs from the
German trenches, the pipings of piccolos and from our broad
lines laughter and Christmas carols. Not a shot was fired.*[1]

Now, we know that eventually fighting resumed between
both sides, but the Christmas truce demonstrates that even in
the most fraught and contentious situations—and it's hard to
get hairier than trench warfare—a shared empathy and a collective will can win out. It's absolutely possible.

In contemporary, daily life, human connection may look
less dramatic. For instance, my friend Christina and her brother
had always been very close, and yet as they grew older, they developed pretty disparate worldviews. In a tense political environment, they frequently sparred. Ultimately, neither was ever
going to convince the other to come around to their point of
view, and they knew it. They would talk, and then they would
each go back to their respective echo chambers. Christina and
her brother did have something in common, though. They
each agreed that vitriol didn't feel very good and that their family was important to them. In the end, they agreed that they
could go into their separate spheres, but that they would hold
a seat at the table for the other. So when Christina next talked
politics with like-minded people, she would say, respectfully,

"You know, my brother sees it differently. If he were here, what he'd say is . . ."

By trying to imagine what he'd say, and vice versa, Christina and her brother were practicing empathy. And their empathy helped them to foster humility, curiosity, and new understandings. By asking what it might be like to inhabit someone else's body, their world, their history, and their worldview, they allowed their own positions to be slightly less rigid, and it helped to take the heat out of their conversations. They didn't necessarily agree, but they respected that they were each coming from a place that was good-hearted. And if a position was less than good-hearted, they were able to articulate why that view created harm or felt oppressive to them without fear of sledgehammer reprisals. Christina and her brother were using their relational tension (literally in this case!) to negotiate a way for them to coexist. They were in dialogue, not debate.

The bottom line is that we can use these insights: 1) relational tension can be a good thing, 2) we have more in common than not, and 3) it's possible to build connection with people by tapping into this commonality and channeling it back into our daily actions. In this way, we travel, more or less, together and in the same general direction. Essentially, we can think about this as a way to point our futures cone from the last chapter like a flashlight toward a distant horizon. We'll all land somewhere along its beam of light—some will be a few millimeters away from the source (still clinging to a *plausible* or *pos-*

sible future, but working on the examining bit), others will be further along (experimenting with *examined desired futures*), but all will be pointed toward and participating in a more brilliant future.

Last, I want to be clear that "finding the others" isn't a naïve endeavor—we have very real divides that require truth, reconciliation, and healing, and we need writers and thinkers and politicians and protestors out advocating for their various causes. We can *be* those writers and thinkers and politicians and protestors. Longpath operates parallel to protest songs, not in opposition to them; "finding the others" simply asks that we also work to find the tones and harmonies that allow all of our voices to come together, in addition to our parts. One does not preclude the other; it enhances it.

Impacting Your Sphere of Influence

We all have a sphere of influence: our colleagues, families, peers, friends, students, communities. Within this sphere, you can communicate a Longpath approach to life and decisions and help steer the shape of that relationship toward things that are of benefit to the future. You can be the honey that attracts the attention of others. Although there are many ways to spark curiosity and engage with other people, we'll talk about four modes of inviting others into the Longpath journey: through our vision, conversation, facilitation, and ways of being.

Through Our Vision

We can bring others alongside by painting visions of the future. A visionary can be an artist, creating abstract visions of new worlds; a political scientist, imagining new forms of governance; a CEO-type, translating a vision into a product or organizational structure; a COO-type, who knows how to put boots on the ground to make a vision reality; or even a member of the PTA, who advocates for a school experience that is devoid of bullying. There are no visioning gatekeepers, and no visioning expertise is required. Simple stories and stick figures work just fine, so long as they can express an idea. If we can help others connect to a vision, reality is not too far behind.

Trekkies will remember that in *Star Trek: The Next Generation*, Picard and Co. were pretty into their PADDs—touchscreen "notepads," which presaged the iPad by a good three decades. They also had video calling years before FaceTime. Steve Jobs was not shy about sharing the show's influence. On introducing the fourth-generation iPhone, he said, "I grew up here in the US with *The Jetsons* and *Star Trek* and communicators, dreaming about video calling, and it's real now!"

Many sci-fi writers, like Isaac Asimov, and the artists at *Star*

Trek envisioned the evolution of our eventual hardware—in the case of the PADD, quite literally. But *Star Trek* also imagined the future of our eventual software, our social evolution, appointing a Black woman to take the helm of a ship. Because we had an example, a representation, of a vision that we could hold in common, we could imagine it—engaging our empathy, futures thinking, and telos along the way—and we could begin to create that sort of reality together. Less than two decades after the fictional Uhura (derived from *uhuru*, the Swahili word for "freedom") took charge of that *Star Trek* vessel, Mae C. Jemison was aboard the space shuttle *Endeavour*. We also have Captain Uhura to thank for a kiss with Captain Kirk, which was in many ways *Star Trek* creator Gene Roddenberry's way of opening the door for normalizing interracial coupling, just a year after the Supreme Court struck down laws in the US banning interracial marriage.

While we can rely on science fiction and a host of other storytellers as means to push the boundaries of what futures can be—from David Bowie's *Ziggy Stardust* to Sun Ra Arkestra's interplanetary exploration of jazz to composers of Afrofuturism—a vision may also be prompted by a garden swap with your neighbors ("my cucumbers for your tomatoes"), pitching a carbon offset plan to your board of directors, establishing a zero-tolerance policy for corporate polluters, or doing away with a standing military force. Such things may or may not manifest, but you've raised the possibility. Just prompting, just by asking a question, you've opened the aperture of possible futures. Next step is finding a way to connect others more deeply to what's possible, to find an empathetic common ground.

Through Our Conversation

Sometimes we can bring others along in ways that are explicit, verbal, and directive. Not everyone will want to sit around and discuss the nature of the universe or the meaning of life with you—shocking, I know—and so every exchange, every dialogue, must begin with mutual consent. Just like Christina and her brother did earlier in this chapter, look for an opening, and then ask for permission to open that window wider. People will have vastly different comfort levels with the subject matters covered in this book—some will be all-in to talk about death and their descendants and how they reckon with their ancestral past, and others will feel much more comfortable talking about the future of sports (hey, now you have Michelle's sports stadium story or my wacky high school groundskeeper anecdote to start an inroad). The point is: Know your audience, meet them where they are, and don't push too far. I might have learned this one the hard way when I talked to my daughter's Girl Scout troop about the future of civilization. They looked at me like I was nuts, and so did their parents.

As you connect with others, should you do so verbally, adopt the approach that someone else's truth is their truth. Your role isn't to convince them to think exactly the way you do. Your role is to explore the commonality between you and to build on that. You can push some boundaries and edge up against the limits of what's comfortable, but your interaction is probably going to be more productive if you're not constantly pushing other people's buttons. Remember, our short-term minds make it hard enough for us to think about far futures; you don't want to exacerbate it by being a mosquito buzzing in someone's ear or drawing blood every two minutes—you'll get swatted or worse!

If you're engaged in dialogue about Longpath, pay attention to its trajectory. While "How did we get here?" has a role, it is not the whole conversation. I'm clearly a proponent of understanding our past and analyzing how it plays into how we think and act now, but don't get stuck there, because it can stop you from progressing beyond debating the minutiae of a cause and effect. See if you can guide the exchange toward "Where are we going?" and "Where do we want to be?" It's a whole other conversational posture.

Also, the conversation doesn't always have to be *explicitly* about Longpath—the word might not even come up. For instance, my friend Horatio attended a meeting at his law firm where the partners discussed their policies about flexible schedules. The conversation very quickly became about logistics, fairness, and office politics, and past grievances were aired and dissected. And so, Horatio brought it back around to what their ultimate goal or aim was. "What is it we want to accomplish?" he asked. "How did we come to assume we all need to be in the office in the first place, and what kind of workplace do we want to be? How do we envision it? What values lie beneath that vision?" He didn't use the word *telos*, but he used the concept as a touchpoint, and in that way changed the scope of conversation from the firm's short-term needs to its Longpath goals.

My friend Jennifer used Longpath, too, without using it, when she had an emotionally charged conversation with her dad. Jennifer and her siblings were throwing her parents a fiftieth anniversary party, and Jennifer's dad was so worried about the logistics being flawed (and thus, on an evolutionary level, hurting his standing within the "clan") that he kept interfering even though Jennifer and her siblings asked him not to. So Jennifer asked him to remember back to when he threw his own parents an anniversary party, how good it felt to give them a gift, and how he might have felt if they had interfered. Then she said, "Think of how you want to feel the night of the party—how you want to look upon and feel about your children, and your grandchildren, and how you want to feel about your wife. And how you want *us*, and your grandkids, to feel about you." She took their interaction from the temporal and the logistical to the emotional, reminding her dad—and herself—of their telos, or ultimate aim.

Through Facilitation

We can bring others along by visioning and communicating futures, but what do we need to do to formalize events or strategies that allow us to Longpath? Well, first, we need to create safe spaces to talk about big things, whether it be strategic planning at the office or estate planning at home. Psychological safety is established when people feel that they can speak up without being punished or humiliated, when no idea or contribution is too outrageous. Facilitators organize settings where there is an equal distribution of power—in everything from the order of who speaks to how the chairs are set around the table . . . or maybe excluding a table altogether.

Environment *matters*. When Google wanted to better understand the forces behind its most effective teams, they found it wasn't expertise or seniority that counted, but a sense of psychological safety among team members. When we establish safe spaces, when we invite diversity and co-create ground rules for open engagement, we will most likely get to that creative third path that benefits everyone.

The organization Death Over Dinner, a supper club that is organized around conversations about death, offers an example of how anyone can facilitate these spaces. It offers guidance about creating a safe space for this hard and incredibly meaningful conversation, and provides prompts to get the party started. And many people will testify that it is a party! You laugh, you cry, you come away feeling connected. Death is a story shared in common. Now, what would happen if one of those Death Over Dinner icebreakers was a question about far-future legacies? Or far-past legacies? How might the experience go even deeper?

Governments, nonprofits, and for-profits can be Longpath facilitators by sponsoring events where a cross-section of the population gets together to vision—and make decisions—together. The island of Aruba did this in 2008, when it engaged some fifty thousand people from Aruban society for the Nos Aruba 2025 project. Together they created a sustainable national strategic plan that took into account what Aruba and its residents had to offer. The process fundamentally changed not only Aruba, but also how its citizens engaged with the government. Hawaii did something similar in the 1970s, and Kansas City recently did, too, though on a much smaller scale. In the latter, the Kauffman Foundation organized a two-day workshop of fifteen residents who held a broad range of perspectives, representing a wide swath of the city. They were asked to co-create a future for a single intersection in Kansas City that had been long divided along racial lines. *Leave perceived limitations behind,* they were told, *and build the future together.*[2]

And, of course, I would be remiss not to mention Longpath.Gather. Longpath Labs hosts gatherings where participants have the opportunity to practice in community, going through exercises much like those described in this book, with a group of others who—while not necessarily like-minded— have a shared interest in talking about the big stuff. In these ways, participants can share, reinforce, and co-create the Longpath narrative. You can check out the latest on these groups at Longpath.org.

Through Our Ways of Being

Finally, our call to Find the Others may actually be a call to Inspire the Others. If I express gratitude to you and you reflect on how good it felt, you may be more likely to express gratitude to someone else. Sometimes those connections don't even involve conversation but rather a nod at the grocery store or a smile when passing in the street. Our ways of being within our sphere of influence have the potential to spark chain reactions.

Through our ways of being, we can create conditions that are conducive to manifesting our telos. If we imagine a world where there's access to books and literacy, for instance, we can start a Free Little Library. If we imagine a world where everyone has access to healthy food, we can start a community garden in food deserts. If we want a world with a little more trust, we show up when we say we will, or we save the last slice of pie, or we watch someone's kid for them, or we offer a dime when someone is short at the grocery store. If we want to reach the other side of the ravine, we can put out a slackline. We never know who might join us.

Think of this strategy like the innate attachment and bonding that happens between babies and their caregivers. Babies can't talk, nor can they understand their caregivers' speech. But it's imperative to development that the baby *understand* that it is cared for. A healthy feeling of attachment helps the baby's brain and nervous system develop optimally, and it helps set the foundation for traits like trust and empathy. Without the language piece, the sense of safety and love that gets communicated to an infant happens through hundreds of micro-expressions and cues: the tone of a voice, the touch of skin on skin, a calm facial expression, responsiveness to distress. These cues may come naturally to caregivers, or they may require some practice at first, but for most people, they become something they just do, their way of being with their child. In the same way, when we start using prosocial cues, we may also need to mind our nonverbal communication. Things like an open stance, a tilt of the head to indicate attentive listening, or putting a phone facedown when someone is talking to you can signal to others that you are a person who is safe to engage with, that you care. When we embody these ways of being, we won't have to work so hard to communicate our goodwill to our neighbor—*even our far-future neighbors!* It will just be what we do.

TAKE A MOMENT TO consider your Lattice of Being, all the lives—past, present, and future—that are connected to your time here on Earth. Which other points on this lattice do you feel most connection with? Which ones do you carry the most influence with? Which ones have relational tensions that are rigid and which ones feel more malleable? What is a Longpath vision that you'd like to share? Perhaps you'd like to choose a point of contact and invite them into conversation. Does your vision change or evolve during your interaction? Maybe you feel comfortable inviting others to join in the exploration of your vision or you'd like to hear about theirs.

I have long been an admirer of the work of the David Lynch Foundation, which uses Transcendental Meditation as a tool to heal traumatic stress and promote resilience. And so I came to learn about Rena Boone, a longtime meditation teacher with the foundation, whose life epitomizes the practice of finding the others. Truth be told, her story epitomizes all of Longpath, so let me start from the beginning.

Rena is a vibrant Black woman who had a rough childhood

and grew up in a family loaded with dysfunction. When she was in college, a professor gave her class an assignment to "describe life," to which Rena answered, "Life is just one damn thing after another."

Rena suspected that life held more, though, and in her search for answers, she found Transcendental Meditation (TM). The practice allowed her to feel peaceful for the first time in her life. From that place of peace, she was able to forgive her parents for her upbringing. "When I think of my parents," she said, "and their parents and what they went through, I have nothing but compassion and love for them and thank them for giving me life." As she moved past her blockages, the inner and outer edges of the Mobius strip came together for Rena. "I think what's inside of us is the ability to love, to be compassionate, the ability to love thy neighbor as thyself," she said. "But how can you love thy neighbor if you don't love thyself? So if you get rid of all of that negativity, all of that toxic stress, just imagine what would be there, what it would be like? Our most intelligent and loving self would emerge."

When Rena had two boys, she turned to raising them as men who would have a healthy mindset, and who would feel that they could go anywhere in the world and feel at home. "I know how important it is to change patterns of behavior, to change thinking, to change paradigms—because those paradigms get transferred to the next generation." Rena also turned to teaching TM, so that others would have access to the tool that made such a difference for her. She has taught the practice for forty years, and now, through the David Lynch Foundation's Center for Resilience, she runs a meditation program in an at-risk community in southeast D.C. Rena has taught TM to students, to help them reduce their stress and achieve their full potential in the classroom, and she has taught TM to those suffering from toxic lifestyles and trauma. "My work is about evolution," she said. "As we evolve, we become more and more who we are. It's about transformation, the full potential of the human race. I am happiest when I am helping others and myself to be all that we can be."

Rena found herself first, and then she found the others. In the process, she touched all four categories from this chapter: She has been a visionary, painting a picture for her students of a more evolved, less stressed humanity; she has started endless conversations about telos, even if she hasn't used the term; she has brought people together in safe spaces, to facilitate growth in the areas that matter most; and her ways of being in the world enact her vision every day. "There are signs of evolution everywhere," she said. "You may not find it on the news—but you will find it in your life. I'm noticing recently how kind people are. I'm always paying attention to kindness when I see it show up, someone taking the time when you walk into a store to say, 'You go ahead.' I'm wired to see that because it uplifts me. And if we're not paying attention, we can miss a lot of good. When we are centered within ourselves it makes it easier to see those golden moments."

After forty years of teaching and daily interactions, the impact of Rena's ripple across interconnected spheres of influence is impossible to quantify. And it's growing every day, across space and time.

The most meaningful Longpath interactions often begin 1–1, but then become 2–1, then 3–1. No, it's not the most efficient method. It would be easier to grab a bullhorn or take out an ad. This quiet way is slow, and it's sometimes messy. It often involves grappling with deeply held beliefs and entrenched behaviors. But it's also how sustainable change happens, in smaller conversations, in smaller interactions, in smaller habits that build in progression. It's these moments that breed longevity, because it's in these moments that we change the defaults of our cultural norms.

So you see, I'm not advocating a loud movement but a subtle shift, a quiet sharing of a new mindset. Now, certainly, if you're in a position to do more, do more. If you can conserve thousands of acres of old-growth forests or pen legislation that ends food insecurity, go for it! But if what you have to offer is managing your daily anxiety so your kids have a better role model than you did, congratulations, you're Longpathing. If you make a point of observing your tone of voice when talking to your loved ones, you're Longpathing. If a birthday reminder for an old friend pops up on your calendar and you call to wish them a good day, that's Longpathing. If you ask, at a meeting, "What are the long-term, next-generation implications of this decision?," that's Longpathing. If you catch yourself arguing with your spouse in front of your kids and stop to think, *What message is this sending them?* that's Longpathing. And if you happen to be reading this behind your desk in the Oval Office and ask yourself, *Will this policy lead to thriving a hundred years from now? A thousand years from now?* that is Longpathing. Set this goal as your stated intention and acknowledge your action as a gift to those who will come after you. If you run into others who experience a similar struggle, see if you can strategize together and distribute your stress more evenly across a support system, or reduce it altogether. Check in periodically to see if you have the capacity to add another goal or another point of contact to your Longpath vision. This is how humanity makes it through its latest rite of passage, its latest iteration and evolution. This is how we become the great ancestors that future generations need us to be.

HAVE YOU FOUND THAT holding a Longpath vision changes anything in your daily life? In the lives of others? What impact do you think your vision will make on generations that will exist a hundred years from now? A thousand years from now? Ten thousand years from now? Can you imagine a history lesson in the far-far-far-future acknowledging this very moment as a great turning point in human trajectory? How does this possibility make you feel? What actions can you commit to that support this potential? Take notes and revise the details of your plans as conditions change.

Epilogue

striking fact about the history of civilization," wrote Hilary Greaves and William MacAskill, philosophers at Oxford University, "is just how early we are in it." They point out that if we reach just a *typical* survival point for mammalian species, we've got some two hundred thousand years to go. We're babies. Infants, really. "If humanity's saga were a novel," Greaves and MacAskill point out, "we would be on the very first page."[1]

Let that perspective of scale sink in one last time. But when it does, don't let it feel daunting or disempowering. Resist any thoughts like *I'm just a speck, what can I do?* A lot of people think the way you change the world is through policy and government, and yes, those avenues are important. Popular culture and its influences are important, too. We talk about these aspects of change all the time, right? But what no one wants to talk about are the human interactions that transpire moment to moment. A police officer's patience shortens a conflict; a board member's extra attention to supply chain builds long-term value; an engineering team's consideration of possible futures leads to less biased artificial intelligence; a school's community garden connects kids to healthy food choices; a citizen's vision for their grandchildren leads them to reject nationalistic ideologies; and a parent's attentive awareness changes how they say goodbye to their kids tomorrow. These moments may feel too slippery, too small to fully capture their significance in a world of Big Data and Big Ideas. But as someone who has been futuring for more than two decades, I can tell you that the thousands of micro-interactions you have every day—be it with others or inside your own head—are what are going to steer this ship of *Homo sapiens* where we want it to go.

Epilogues are typically where the author has the last word, where they strike just the right note to leave readers with an imprint of their vision. I want to flip this epilogue on its head, though. I want it to end with you. What if you could write a note to the future to be read to everyone who lives in it? Write your thoughts about what the most important thing in life is, the wisdom you most want to pass on, or maybe a wish or benediction that you want to offer them. Let the words come from your heart.

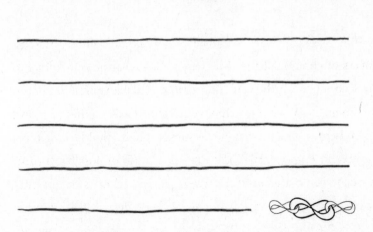

Now bring your words to life. Live that note. Become the great ancestor the future needs you to be.

[THE END. OR . . . THE BEGINNING.]

LONGPATH MEGATRENDS

SOCIAL & CULTURAL SHIFTS

- DECLINE of TRADITIONAL GROUPS & ORGANIZATIONS
- GLOBALIZATION of IDEAS & NARRATIVES
- RISE of DIGITAL CULTURE & SOCIAL NETWORKS
- RISE in STATUS & POWER of WOMEN

DEMOGRAPHIC SHIFTS

- GROWTH of the MILLENNIAL GENERATION
- BOOMERS RE-BOOMING
- URBANIZATION EVERYWHERE
- RISE of the NEW RACIAL & ETHNIC MAJORITY

SCIENCE & TECH DEVELOPMENTS

- ADVANCEMENTS in BIO-ENGINEERING
- RADICAL TRANSPARENCY & RISE in BIG DATA
- BREAKTHROUGHS in ENERGY RESOURCES
- 0101 of EVERYTHING • UBIQUITOUS INTELLIGENCE

ENVIRONMENTAL DYNAMICS

- CLIMATE-BASED DISEASE SPREAD
- CLIMATE-BASED MIGRATION
- CLIMATE CHANGE & RESOURCE SCARCITY

ECONOMIC SHIFTS

- MULTI-POLAR GLOBAL ECONOMIC ORDER
- DISAGGREGATED & DISTRIBUTED WORK
- RISING INCOME DISPARITY

POLITICAL DYNAMICS

- DECLINE in TRADITIONAL INSTITUTIONAL POWER
- NEW TURF WARS

Journal Pages

- book for upper MG ∞
- picture book
- Yale Happiness Course
- Pushing the boundaries of + what's possible
- Voros Cone
- Workbooks
- line of Long Path workbooks?

Journal Pages

Journal Pages

Journal Pages

Journal Pages

Journal Pages

Acknowledgments

I have been blessed for more than four decades with the good fortune of being surrounded by family, friends, and colleagues who have helped me in ways big and small. A full list of all those who have helped me along my path would require a second volume, so what follows is an all-too-brief list.

While obvious, I would not be here, as I am, without the deepest of belief in me held by my mother and father. Although my father, Raul, passed away during my freshman year of college and my mother, Susan, during the earliest stages of this book's writing, their wisdoms are on every page. Thanks to my sisters, Deborah and Liza, for all that it takes to raise a younger brother and help guide when the path is not so clear.

Thanks to Jennifer and Jonathan Soros, the earliest of supporters of Longpath Labs, and whose dedication to future generations knows no bounds.

Of course I have benefitted from the earliest of beliefs in this book by my agent Howard Yoon and my editor at HarperOne, Anna Paustenbach, without whom this book would still be a series of notes somewhere in the cloud. The team at HarperOne who helped put this all together and onto a shelf near you includes Sun Paik, Leda Scheintaub, Joy O'Meara, and Adrian Morgan. Brooke Budner created the book's beautiful illustrations. I was lucky enough to have Longpath's inaugural director of research, Dr. Kim Streeter, provide both early comments and ongoing insights across every page. My writing spirit-guide and counselor was the indomitable Jenna Land Free. Without her helping hand and mind, this book you hold in your hands would not be manifest.

Friends and colleagues who have been guiding lights and the strongest of supporters along the path to getting this book into the world include Nathan Arbitman, Hollie-Russon Gilman, Lou Caballero, Douglas Rushkoff, Michelle Moore, Kathryn Murdoch, Jeff Stoike, Anna Burger, Adam Bly, Jonathan Barzilay, Liz Frierich, Ruth Baldwin, Amanda Silver, Jeremy Wertheim, Dan Liechty, Scott Osman, Aaron Graben, Lindsay Litowitz, Mike Brooks, Emma Goldberg, Nils Gilman, Tiffany Shlain, Mik Moore, Jennifer Hoos-Rothberg, Rabbi David Ingber, David Zweig, Bruce Feiler, Ryan Senser, Rabbi Sharon Brous, Ai-Jen Poo, Ytasha Womack, Courtney Martin, David DeSteno,

Jamil Zaki, Hal Hershfield, Hahrie Han, Nina Mazar, Prof. Jerry Sanders, Rena Boone, Max Klau, and Doug Sundheim.

Titanic influences on my thinking come courtesy of Herbert Marcuse, J. Krishnamurti, Buckminster Fuller, Ernest Becker, Isaac Asimov, Octavia Butler, Marty Seligman, Alan Watts, and Ursula K. Le Guin.

And yes, there would be no Longpath, no path whatsoever, without the support, care, love, feeding, and lifelong friendship and belief in me of my wife and partner, Sharon Goldman Wallach.

Notes

Chapter 1: Living

1. Edelman, "Edelman Trust Barometer 2021," accessed August 27, 2021, https://www.edelman.com/trust/2021-trust-barometer.
2. United States National Intelligence Council, "Global Trends 2040," McLean, VA: Office of the Director of National Intelligence, 2021, https://www.dni.gov/files/ODNI/documents/assessments/Global Trends_2040.pdf.
3. "Millions Tumble Out of the Middle Class," *Bloomberg* video, April 7, 2021, https://www.bloomberg.com/news/videos/2021-04-07/millions-tumble-out-of-the-middle-class-video.
4. Edelman, "Edelman Trust Barometer 2021."
5. Shane McFeely and Ryan Pendell, "What Workplace Leaders Can Learn from the Real Gig Economy," *Gallup*, August 16, 2018, https://www.gallup.com/workplace/240929/workplace-leaders-learn-real-gig-economy.aspx.
6. Ziauddin Sardar, "Welcome to Postnormal Times," *Futures* 42, no. 5 (June 2010): 435–44, doi: 10.1016/j.futures.2009.11.028.
7. Ilya Prigogine and Isabelle Stengers, *Order Out of Chaos: Man's New Dialogue with Nature* (New York: Bantam, 1984).
8. Similar examples exist in how the Ming Dynasty fell in China in the 1500s and even in the downfall of the Mayans in the 900s.

9. If you're interested in guesstimating your own number of descendants, check out familyrecordfinder.com/descendants.html. The formula used is $=x^1+x^2 \ldots x^n$, where n=generations and x=children.

10. Julie Beck, "Where Life Has Meaning: Poor Religious Countries," *Atlantic,* January 10, 2014, https://www.theatlantic.com/health/archive/2014/01/where-life-has-meaning-poor-religious-countries/282949/.

Chapter 2: Changing

1. In a recent survey of six hundred corporate executives, two-thirds of them felt pressure to focus on short-term results. Jonathan Bailey et al., "Short-termism: Insights from Business Leaders," Focusing Capital on the Long Term, January 2014, https://www.fcltglobal.org/wp-content/uploads/20140123-mck-quarterly-survey-results-for-fclt-org_final.pdf.

2. Manda Mahoney, "The Subconscious Mind of the Consumer (And How to Reach It)," *Working Knowledge,* Harvard Business School, January 13, 2003, https://hbswk.hbs.edu/item/the-subconscious-mind-of-the-consumer-and-how-to-reach-it. The 80 percent came from here but is not specifically sourced: Michael Levine, "Logic and Emotion," *Psychology Today,* July 12, 2012, https://www.psychologytoday.com/gb/blog/the-divided-mind/201207/logic-and-emotion.

3. Teressa Iezzi, "No Future: Present Shock and Why Our Now-Fixation Has Changed Everything from Advertising to Politics," *Fast Company,* July 8, 2015, https://www.fastcompany.com/1682643/no-future-present-shock-and-why-our-now-fixation-has-changed-everything-from-advertising-to.

4. Yohan J. John, "The 'Streetlight Effect': A Metaphor for Knowledge and Ignorance," *3 Quarks Daily,* March 21, 2016, https://3quarksdaily.com/3quarksdaily/2016/03/the-streetlight-effect-a-metaphor-for-knowledge-and-ignorance.html.

5. Trevor Haynes, "Dopamine, Smartphones & You: A Battle for Your Time," *Science in the News,* Harvard University Graduate School of

Arts and Sciences, May 1, 2018, https://sitn.hms.harvard.edu/flash /2018/dopamine-smartphones-battle-time/.

6. American Museum of Natural History, "Human Population Through Time," YouTube video, November 4, 2016, https://www .youtube.com/watch?v=PUwmA3Q0_OE.

7. Carol S. Dweck, *Mindset: The New Psychology of Success* (New York: Ballantine, 2007).

8. David DeSteno, personal correspondence with author, June 2021.

9. David DeSteno, "The Kindness Cure," *Atlantic*, July 21, 2015, https://www.theatlantic.com/health/archive/2015/07/mindful ness-meditation-empathy-compassion/398867/.

10. Shanyu Kates and David DeSteno, "Gratitude Reduces Consumption of Depleting Resources," *Emotion* (December 28, 2020), doi: 10.1037/emo0000936.

11. TEDx Talks, "We're experiencing an empathy shortage, but we can fix it together | Jamil Zaki | TEDxMarin," YouTube video, October 18, 2018, https://www.youtube.com/watch?v=-DspKSYxYDM.

12. Erika Weisz et al., "Building Empathy Through Motivation-Based Interventions," *Emotion* (November 19, 2020), doi: 10.1037/emo 0000929.

Chapter 3: Practicing

1. J. Krishnamurti—Official Channel, "Audio | J. Krishnamurti— Amsterdam 1969—Public Talk 2—How Is Conditioning to Be Understood?" YouTube video, November 24, 2020, https://www.you tube.com/watch?v=279RfTu0gKY. Content reproduced with permission. For more information about J. Krishnamurti (1895–1986), see: www.jkrishnamurti.org.

2. Cameron Hewitt, "Unwanted Statues? A Modest Proposal, from Hungary," *Rick Steves' Europe,* June 18, 2020, https://blog.ricksteves .com/cameron/2020/06/hungary-statues/.

3. Bryan Stevenson, discussion with Rabbi Sharon Brous for Yom Kippur, September 2020.

4. Christina Chwyl, Patricia Chen, and Jamil Zaki, "Beliefs About Self-Compassion: Implications for Coping and Self-Improvement,"

Notes

Personality and Social Psychology Bulletin 47, no. 9 (September 2021): 1327–42, doi: 10.1177/0146167220965303.

5. Ernest Becker, *The Denial of Death* (New York: Free Press, 1973), 26.

6. Atul Gawande, *Being Mortal: Medicine and What Matters in the End* (New York: Picador, 2017).

7. Michael Hebb, *Let's Talk About Death (Over Dinner)* (New York: DaCapo Lifelong Books, 2018).

8. TED, "Laura Carstensen: Older People Are Happier," YouTube video, April 9, 2012, https://www.youtube.com/watch?v=7gkdzkVbuVA.

9. Terri Hansen, "How the Iroquois Great Law of Peace Shaped U.S. Democracy," PBS.org, December 17, 2018, https://www.pbs.org/native-america/blogs/native-voices/how-the-iroquois-great-law-of-peace-shaped-us-democracy/#1.

10. Daniel Gilbert, *Stumbling on Happiness* (New York: Knopf, 2006).

11. John Tierney, "Why You Won't Be the Person You Expect to Be," *New York Times*, January 3, 2013, https://www.nytimes.com/2013/01/04/science/study-in-science-shows-end-of-history-illusion.html.

12. Emily Pronin, Christopher Y. Olivola, and Kathleen A. Kennedy, "Doing Unto Future Selves As You Would Do Unto Others: Psychological Distance and Decision Making," *Personality and Social Psychology Bulletin*, 34, no. 2 (February 2008): 224–36, doi: 10.1177/0146167207310023.

13. Arnaud D'Argembeau and Martial Van der Linden, "Emotional Aspects of Mental Time Travel," *Behavioral and Brain Sciences*, 30, no. 3 (June 2007): 320–21, doi: 10.1017/S0140525X07002051.

14. Debora Bettiga and Lucio Lamberti, "Future-Oriented Happiness: Its Nature and Role in Consumer Decision-Making for New Products," *Frontiers in Psychology*, 11, no. 929 (May 2020), doi: 10.3389/fpsyg.2020.00929.

15. Yoshio Kamijo et al., "Negotiating with the Future: Incorporating Imaginary Future Generations into Negotiations," *Sustainability Science*, 12, no. 3 (May 2017): 409–20, doi: 10.1007/s11625-016-0419-8.

16. John Koetsier, "Why Every Amazon Meeting Has at Least 1 Empty Chair," Inc.com, April 5, 2018, https://www.inc.com/john-koetsier/why-every-amazon-meeting-has-at-least-one-empty-chair.html.

Chapter 4: Creating

1. Centers for Disease Control and Prevention, National Center for Health Statistics, "Death Rates Due to Suicide and Homicide among Persons Aged 10–24: United States, 2000–2017," Sally C. Curtain, M.A. and Melonie Heron, Ph.D., NCHS Data Brief no. 352 (Hyattsville, MD, October 2019), https://www.cdc.gov/nchs/data/data briefs/db352-h.pdf.

2. Peter Daszak et al., "Infectious Disease Threats: A Rebound to Resilience," *Health Affairs*, 40, no. 2 (January 2021): 204–11, doi: 10.1377/hlthaff.2020.01544.

3. "Russia 'Meddled in All Big Social Media' around US Election," *BBC News* online, December 18, 2018, https://www.bbc.com/news/technology-46590890.

4. Roy F. Baumeister et al., "Everyday Thoughts in Time: Experience Sampling Studies of Mental Time Travel," *Personality and Social Psychology Bulletin*, 46, no. 12 (December 2020): 1631–48, doi: 10.1177/0146167220908411.

5. "Wedding Services in the US—Market Size 2005–2027," IBIS World, April 29, 2021, https://www.ibisworld.com/industry-statistics/market-size/wedding-services-united-states/.

6. John Lane, *Timeless Simplicity* (Cambridge, UK: Green Books, 2001).

7. Laurie Santos, "Laurie Santos, Yale Happiness Professor, on 5 Things That Will Make You Happier," *Newsweek*, January 8, 2021, https://www.newsweek.com/2021/01/08/issue.html.

8. Xu Guifeng et al., "Twenty-Year Trends in Diagnosed Attention-Deficit/Hyperactivity Disorder Among US Children and Adolescents, 1997–2016," *JAMA Network Open*, 1, no. 4 (August 2018), doi: 10.1001/jamanetworkopen.2018.1471.

9. Viktor Frankl, *Man's Search for Meaning* (Boston: Beacon Press, 2006), 104.

10. Barbara L. Fredrickson and Marcial Losada, "Positive Affect and the Complex Dynamics of Human Flourishing," *American Psychologist*, 60 no. 7 (October 2005): 678–86, doi: 10.1037/0003-066X.60.7.678.

11. Felicia Huppert and Timothy So, "Flourishing across Europe: Application of a New Conceptual Framework for Defining Well-Being,"

Social Indicators Research, 110, no. 3 (February 2013): 837–61, doi: 10.1007/s11205-011-9966-7

12. TED, "The 'Dementia Village' That's Redefining Elder Care | Yvonne van Amerongen," YouTube video, April 8, 2019, https://www.youtube.com/watch?v=YSZhrxOkBZI.

Chapter 5: Flourishing

1. Mike Dash, "The Story of the WWI Christmas Truce," *Smithsonian Magazine* online, December 23, 2011, https://www.smithsonianmag.com/history/the-story-of-the-wwi-christmas-truce-11972213/.

2. Chun-Yin San, "Democratising the Future: How Do We Build Inclusive Visions of the Future?," *Nesta*, December 20, 2017, https://www.nesta.org.uk/blog/democratising-the-future-how-do-we-build-inclusive-visions-of-the-future/.

3. Ewing Marion Kauffman Foundation, "At the Corner of the Future: Kansas City's World Building Pilot," Kauffman.org video, July 26, 2018, https://www.kauffman.org/currents/at-the-corner-of-the-future/.

Epilogue

1. Hilary Greaves and William MacAskill, "The Case for Strong Longtermism," University of Oxford Global Priorities Institute, accessed August 29, 2021, https://globalprioritiesinstitute.org/wp-content/uploads/2019/Greaves_MacAskill_The_Case_for_Strong_Long termism.pdf.

About the Author

Ari ben Zion Wallach is the founder and executive director of Longpath Labs, an initiative focused on ensuring humanity flourishes on an ecologically thriving planet Earth for centuries to come.

Wallach's TED talk on Longpath has been viewed more than 2.5 million times and translated into nineteen languages. From the UN Refugee Agency and the US State Department to Auburn Seminary and the marriage equality start-up Friend Factor, Wallach has helped organizations envision the futures they want and the strategies needed to get them there for more than twenty years. Wallach was the cofounder of the 2008 presidential initiative "The Great Schlep with Sarah Silverman" and most previously hosted *Fast Company* magazine's *Fast Company Futures with Ari Wallach*. As adjunct associate professor at Columbia University's School of International and Public Affairs, he has lectured on innovation, AI, and the futures of public policy.

He has served as an expert panel review judge for the Racial Equity 2030 global challenge as well as for the MacArthur Foundation's $100 million grant challenge. He is a graduate of the University of California, Berkeley, a 2003 Coro Fellow in New York City, and a member of Harvard's Gettysburg Project for Civic Engagement. Ari lives in the Hudson Valley with his wife, three children, and their labradoodle, Ozzie.

To find out more and get involved please visit www.Longpath.org.

LONGPATH